DEMY
MASCULINITY

DEMYSTIFYING
MASCULINITY

Matthew Lloyd Collins

Another Quality Book Published By:
LEGACY BOOK PUBLISHING
1883 Lee Road, Winter Park, FL 32789
www.LEGACYBOOKPUBLISHING.com

Demystifying Masculinity

Published by:
LEGACY Book Publishing
1883 Lee Road
Winter Park, Florida 32789
www.LegacyBookPublishing.com

Printed in the United States, First Printing
ISBN: 978-1-947718-62-3

Cover Design by Gabriel H. Vaughn
Managing Editor: Amanda Molina

“It is easier to build strong children than to repair broken men.”

—Frederick Douglass

PROCLAMATION TO THE WORLD

Problems of violence, low achievement, and overall waywardness plague boys and men today. Governmental, nonprofit, and religious institutions have proven insufficient to address said concerns. It is incumbent upon the men currently walking the earth to teach, mentor, and serve successive generations.

#MakingMenWorkshops
#TheAwakenedManWorkshops

Acknowledgements

I acknowledge Gabriel Vaughn, President of Legacy Book Publishing out of Winter Park, Florida, for his cover art design and overall artistic project vision. Additionally, I would like to acknowledge the eagle eye editing artistry of Amanda Molina. Virginia Wills, my childhood vision has become manifest.

Preface

You were drawn to this book. The title. The cover art. Something pulled you in. Perhaps you are the parent or guardian of a boy, or you might be a young man who was gifted this book. If so, thank the gifter. It is just as likely that you are an adult male seeking self-improvement. Grown men should read this book cover to cover. Some, more than once.

Whatever it was, welcome. Jettison your groupthink hats. Don your critical thinking sombreros. This will be a different type of ride. Buckle up as we embark on deconstructing the single biggest pressing problem facing us today: raising unhealthy boys into broken men.

It is high time for this discussion. Do not shoot the messenger. Without equivocation, I support the equal rights of women. By that very definition, I am a feminist. Let me be clear. The lessons and exercises contained here are equally curative for all human beings, irrespective of the gender continuum.

Onward,

Dr. Matthew Lloyd Collins
(Circa the Genesis of The Roaring 2020s)

Dr. Collins teaches "Making Men Workshops" for boys and "The Awakened Man Workshops" for adult men. Workshops are offered both face-to-face and online. For workshop registration and one-on-one coaching, contact Dr. Collins: at dmlcshow@gmail.com or 267-713-2177.

Table of Contents

Introduction

Toxic Masculinity

As a theoretical construct, the phrase toxic masculinity is used to label the stratospheric levels of hyperbolic violence, emotional unavailability, sexual aggression, and status obsession inherent within the social construction of the male gender role.

Toxic masculinity has been rapidly deployed, with increased frequency as of late, to describe a wide gamut of statements, actions, and behaviors ranging from the innocuous frat boy prank to criminal allegations of sexual impropriety, felonious battery, and even murder.

Once upon a time, but not so long ago, toxic masculinity was an utterance heard only on college campuses, usually in the basement of the social sciences building where the women's studies courses were held. That is not the case today.

You can barely turn on the news these days without hearing some mentioning of toxic masculinity. In contemporary urban dictionary parlance: **toxic masculinity is a catchall explanation for a wide variety of violent acts, misogynistic statements, and the multitude of mannish shenanigans of the many stripes.**

However, let it be clear that *toxic masculinity* and *masculinity* are two very different constructs. All masculinity is not toxic. Therefore, all masculinity need not be extinguished. Pathologizing all masculinity leads us down a very slippery slope.

Ready for an inconvenient truth? Toxic thoughts, utterances, and behaviors are in no way limited to the realm of boys and men. Nevertheless, the ignominious brand of toxic masculinity is vitriolically cast upon any masculine-leaning figure who happens to be caught in the crosshairs of the latest social media-propagated crisis of the day.

Much like the charge of racism, the accusations of being toxically masculine are as overplayed as a bad 1980s song. "Never gonna give you up. Never gonna let you down. Never gonna run around and desert you" (Rick Astley, 1987). You are truly showing your age if you remember Dick Spatsley. Young bucks, YouTube him.

Yet – laying it on thick here – obsessive, and often breathless, television and social media reports of toxic masculinity have elucidated the multitude of very real challenges facing both boys and men today. Very real challenges are serving up very real consequences in very real time.

Without question, toxic masculinity has reached crisis proportions in the Western world today. Moreover, quite admittedly, the construct of toxic masculinity houses many kernels of truth. These kernels of truth bear repeating with the support of much more research and thoughtful analysis in our national discourse.

The tsunami of recent charges of toxic masculinity is a red flag for society at large. Many boys and men in the United States are indeed in crisis. Yet, within such crises, opportunities await. Some of the greatest opportunities are often born out of the reconceptualization of such crises.

Prophetically, Tupac Shakur stated, "It is time to change the way we eat, change the way we live, and change the way we treat each other. You see the old way wasn't working, so it's on us to do what we gotta do, to survive" (1998).

In retrospect, the prescience of that artist's words is nothing short of astounding.

Axiomatically, this book is grounded upon the notion that toxic masculinity exists. Taking Shakur's admonishments to heart, this work provides educative elaboration and analysis on the "Garbage In/Garbage Out" (or "GIGO") inculcative programming that has molded generations of boys and men.

Proceeding with the presupposition that toxic masculinity absolutely exists, it is also quite logical, in this dualistic reality, to propose that a corresponding counterpart to the concept of toxic masculinity must also exist.

The diametrically opposed counterpart to *toxic masculinity* is the concept of *divine masculinity*. Never heard of it? I'm not surprised. Much of the understanding of divine masculinity has been removed from the Earth at this time.

Successive waves of public policy dawning in the twentieth century have incentivized the banishment of the father figure from the familial household environment. The supposedly unintended consequences of those perverse public policy incentives have been both shocking and tragic. In short, the extended familial living arrangement has been eliminated, setting the stage for the rise of the latchkey kid household that has further devolved into homes in which the electronics are now raising the children.

Unfortunately, we still have the propensity to look outside ourselves toward imaginary external forces – whether they be governmental, religious, or other – to show us how to correct and counterbalance the toxically masculine social environment we have collectively allowed to flourish. Going forward, we cannot continue to look outside ourselves for a solution to the toxically masculine milieu quagmire that is besetting America today.

Wake up, folks. The current societal structure and the institutions therein, backed by the contemporaneous political, theater-based public policies, have not the power to inculcate and instill the values and virtues that we should expect from our fellow citizens, irrespective of their gender identification.

Teaching such useful and appropriate values, which lead to virtuous behaviors in boys and men down the road, is not the responsibility of the government nor the school system. Despite their often hyperbolic, self-perceived mastery of public policy-making and administrative prowess, the results are in. These institutions are simply not up for the job. This is our responsibility.

In this age, there is much casting of blame, but very few solutions are offered. Moving forward, we must use our own hands. Playing the "victim card" is a short-term solution. It simply will not work for the long haul. There is a window of truth opening for the world. Take advantage of this exposure to higher vibrational ideas, theories, and concepts. The purpose of this work is healing.

There are myriad societal, political, economic, and – dare I write, spiritual – forces working in an intricate coagulative to synergistically suppress the understanding of divine masculinity on the Earth today. This has been done for a myriad of reasons. The lowest common denominator, which we could all see from space if we were truly looking, is economic profiteering. The best hiding place is often in plain sight.

Yet, it does not behoove us at this stage of the game to conceptualize ourselves as the victims of contemporary or, worse yet, *historical* circumstances. We must now recognize the kernels of truth embodied within the concept of toxic masculinity for what they are. We must meet those kernels of truth head-on with solution-rich ideas aimed toward the healing of both boys and men, as well as society at large.

Remember this fact: Boys and men are not born congenitally toxic. That fact is often lost in this age of contemporary contentiousness fueled by deleteriously driven division, and toxic, social-fabric-tearing programming. Ladies and gentlemen, contrary to the indictment of many talking-head pundits, toxic masculinity is not at all a birth defect. All human beings are of the Creator. Boys and men are human beings. Therefore, boys and men are of the Creator.

Backbiting, argumentation, and even righteous indignation are the old way. This book presents the new way. The higher vibrational path forward. Operating from the basis of strikingly disparate assumptions in comparative juxtaposition with the old ways encapsulated in what I will now refer to as the "proverbs of masculinity."

The Proverbs of Masculinity: "Take it Like a Man," "The Strong, Silent Type," & "Boys Don't Cry"

A proverb is a short, pithy idea, phrase, or statement encapsulating a popularly accepted notion of shared collective reality. Three of the more popular proverbs addressing masculinity are "Take it like a man", "The strong, silent type", and, of course, the always overplayed, "Boys don't cry." What does it even mean to "Take it like a man"?

In the 1970s and 1980s, it was quite common to hear parents utter, "Take it like a man," when boys would skin a knee on the pavement or get roughed up on the playing field. In that context, "Take it like a man" meant to shake off the injury and get your hind parts back into the game. After thirty years of programming that puts garbage into a system, you have a system that gets a garbage output (GIGO).

"My chest hurts. Well, I should take it like a man." No. Report to the nearest emergency room on the double if you are suffering from unusual, sudden, severe chest pain. Do not attempt to "Take it like a man." You may end up taking it like a dead man.

All too often, boys and men in our society shy away from medical doctors. Ignoring health problems while continuously gluttonizing themselves on "CRAP Frankenfood." The very same CRAP Frankenfood known to be strongly correlated with the preponderance of largely preventable physical illnesses besetting the lion's share of boys and men in America today.

From a different angle, the "Take it like a man" proverbial expression could be interpreted to connote that it is not at all manly to express oneself emotionally or to talk about one's feelings. Hence, according to that logic, "real men" do not whine, wail, or complain about any physical or emotional malaise, discomfort, or pain. Nope. They are expected to pull themselves up by their bootstraps, to carry on with the mission.

How ridiculous!

That is all, of course, complete and total malarkey. Boys and men should feel free to discuss physical, health-related, and emotional concerns with others without feeling emasculated in any manner, shape, or form.

Do not be hoodwinked. Eat whole foods, pursue holistic health well-being, and live joyously free from such aforementioned communicative limitations. "Take it like a man" is an antiquated proverbial adage. It is not serving your highest interests today. Jettison it like a moldy hot potato covered in dog feces. You don't need it.

The next masculinity proverb up for deconstruction is "The strong, silent type." Recently I overheard a conversation while in line at the market between two millennial-aged women.

Millennial woman one inquired: "What is the new guy you met on Tinder like?"

Millennial woman two replied: "You know, he is the strong, silent type."

Hearing the mindless repetition of such a tired, platitudinous utterance made me cringe. I thought, "Well, that young man in question is obviously adhering to certain programmatic notions about what it means to be a man. He is portraying himself to be 'The strong, silent, type.' His time is limited with that fake narrative. His foibles, intricacies, and neurotic, fearful self-loathing will inevitably boil up to the surface." There simply comes a breaking point where the young man cannot keep up the façade any longer.

Quite likely, by next week's market session, the story will have evolved.

Millennial woman two will be stating: "We went out downtown Wednesday night. His buddies were all there. He acted differently around them. One of his fraternity brothers drank a bit too much, leaned in, and tried to kiss me on the neck as we were leaving the bar. Tinder boy attacked his frat brother with such enormous violence that the police got involved. He kept texting me. I blocked him on Instagram and Snapchat. He is like a toxic male to the core."

Don't pretend to be "The strong, silent type," then lose your bearing. Your fear-based, sleeper-cell insecurities are conveniently resting beneath the surface of your subconscious, standing entirely at the ready to rear their ugly heads. You will look like a damn fool in the eyes of the world, ruining your day or even the rest of your life (if convicted/jailed).

Be yourself from day one. Do not put up façades. Inevitably, they fall, typically at the most inconvenient times imaginable.

Be honest with yourself. Be polite, cordial, and respectful with all other human beings you encounter on your daily travels.

You don't have to be "The strong, silent type," or any other type, for that matter. Ignore such programming. It is not serving your highest interest today. You will do well to kick the idea of "The strong, silent type" to the curb.

Now, inching forward, let us embark and set forth to take apart the last of the antiquated and inherently sexist proverbial sayings about masculinity. That final proverbial adage on the deconstructive hit list is the infamous "Boys don't cry."

Hey, all of you righteous MTV 1980s music fans out there. Do any of you remember the band The Cure and their 1980 hit song, "Boys Don't Cry"? The lyrics go, "I tried to laugh about it; cover it up with lies; I tried to laugh about it; Hiding the tears in my eyes; 'cause boys don't cry" (The Cure, 1980).

Often, musical and other forms of artistic free expression mimic the constructions of social reality. These are the social constructions that lay the groundwork for the normative acceptable societal rules that many of us opt into, either consciously or less so, regarding gender differentiation responses in the context of various events and stimuli.

"Boys don't cry," by default, is often the unwritten rule. When boys and men reach out to speak to others about their feelings, they are often met with low vibrational and often virulently negative responses and comments, such as "What, are you a girl?" or "Put some Vagisil on it." That needs to end.

Rise up. Elevate your consciousness. Raise your vibration. Do not allow yourself to bottle up emotions. Do not allow for the creation of energetic whirlpools of worry in your human bodily vessel. They soon become physical ailments. Develop connections instead.

Find a trustworthy other who will listen attentively and provide sage advice for your given situation, based in experience and wisdom. Boys and men should seek mentors in the game of life. Human beings cry. Boys and men are human beings. Therefore, boys and men cry.

Awaken. Resist the programming being fed to you by Hollywood, the pharmaceutical industrial complex (PIC), and the various sports corporations as well as tech-giant, oligarch-ruled social media. Social media is chock-full of misinformation. Often, worse yet, disinformation.

Westerners have been bamboozled into making poor health, financial, and behavioral decisions. We have been hornswoggled all around, and the story continues to unfold. It is time for us to wake up and realize that much of what we have been inculcated and programmed to believe is no longer serving our highest interest. Sex and sexuality are no exception. We need a thorough, deconstructive analysis of "the cocksmanization culture."

The Cocksmanization Culture

A "cocksman" is a man renowned for his sexual accomplishments and known far and wide for his stratospheric virility. According to the cocksmanization culture, the wealthiest men, who attract the most beautiful women society has to offer, have attained the very pinnacle of the encapsulation of masculine success. As an umbrella term, the "cocksmanization culture" is the totality of the societal programming and focuses primarily upon the aforementioned misguided thematic message. Nevertheless, boys and men in Western society are steeped in the cocksmanization culture's lies from the cradle onward. It is time for a new understanding of masculine success and the proper concomitant usage of divine masculine sexuality.

From the time of my early childhood in the 1970s and 1980s, it was evident that the society at large had a real admiration for men with good looks, charisma, athletic abilities, and especially the loot to attract the most beautiful women.

Back in my young heyday, prominent cocksmen included the likes of eminent baller and ladies man, Earvin "Magic" Johnson. Who could ever forget the mustached, machismo television star himself, Magnum P.I., for whom the women swooned? Without question, honorable mention would have to go out to the ever-so-smooth Detective Shaft, who always had the foxy ladies on payphone standby! And also of course to the "shaken, not stirred" preeminent connoisseur of the feminine form himself: Mr. 007, James Bond.

Looking back, none of the aforementioned male cinematic and celebrity heroes of my childhood represented healthy, useful, or appropriate examples of how boys and men should interact with girls and women. Beware. Danger, Will Robinson! The old programming regarding getting rich and bedding down a harem of hotties should now be gone with the wind. Words and actions grounded in such toxic programming are simply not tolerated in today's society. Not as they were in the past. The days of slapping a pretty young waitress on the hind parts after referring to her as "little lady" are over!

Thank goodness. That behavior is neither useful nor appropriate in any way, shape, or form. Oppositely, it is both demeaning and humiliating.

Wake up, gentlemen. Today, boys and men live in the age of the #MeToo era, wherein such abhorrent and irresponsibly egregious sexual misconduct is no longer accepted. It will no longer be overlooked. As it should not be.

There is tremendous collective anger that some call righteous indignation on the part of many women over the gender-based transgressions of yesteryear. There is no doubt that women and girls have been treated as second-class citizens by our male forebearers. Yet, the boys and men of today are in no way responsible for such past transgressions. No matter.

There are a multitude of groups, political officials, community activists, academic Ph.D. experts, and a whole cast of cable news talking head political so-called "journalist" pundits who continuously project their often misguided views on masculinity onto the rest of us without any mentioning or recognition of the masculine divine.

Boys and men today are under the microscope. Society has become far less forgiving when it comes to the misuse of sexual power and influence. Just ask R. Kelly, Matt Lauer, or Harvey Weinstein. Yet, the toxic programming has not changed. The cocksmanization culture continues to provide boys and men with horribly inappropriate role model programming examples. Awaken. Do not fall victim to the cocksmanization culture programming conundrum. It is a trap.

The cocksmanization cultural programming is not meant to serve your best interest. Further elaboration on the cocksmanization cultural programming will be provided in chapter one addressing sacred sexuality. Pay close attention to the section on avoiding the porn trap. It just may save your life!

Another area of programming disinformation targeting both boys and men and serving to mold societal perception of the masculine in a self-deprecating, cancerous, self-fulfilling prophesy is referred to as "The Homer Simpsonization of Men."

The Homer Simpsonization of Men

The antiquated proverbs of masculinity, as well as the cocksmanization culture, are mere byproducts of a time long gone when a man like Ward Cleaver – from the hit show of the late 1950s and early 1960s, *Leave it to Beaver* – was the strong male head of the household, protector of the domiciliary realm, and purveyor of knowledge and understanding to his children.

June Cleaver, Ward's lovely wife, joyously cleaned the familial home each episode, donning an impeccably ironed dress with a tasteful pearl necklace. Her hair was always immaculately coiffured. June was a delight. Even during my childhood, that hyperbolically hypermasculine and unmistakably misogynistic way of living had fallen way out of style.

By the end of the 1980s, as I was graduating from high school, the media had stopped exclusively portraying men as the authoritative, familial commander-in-chief like Ward Cleaver was, or as the best spies in the business like James Bond was.

By that time, the entertainment industrial complex (EIC) had shifted the spotlight to a far less impressive cast of characters, such as Al Bundy and Homer Simpson. Bundy was the consummately inept, toxically masculine father figure on the late 1980s show titled *Married with Children.* Simpson was the cartooned caricature combination of the absolute worst qualities of toxic masculinity conjoined with a high dosage of puerile imbecility.

If you seek a nincompoop dad with a spare tire belly, one living straight out of low cache, in possession of no definite real-life purpose, you are in the right room. Look no further than the frequencies of indolence, oblivious ineptitude, and overall low vibrational stupidity of the likes of both Al Bundy and Homer Simpson.

Both of those fictional male characters were portrayed as being inferior to their female spouses intellectually, morally, and spiritually. Moreover, the two characters had less life savviness than even their young children.

Now, I get it. Don't get me wrong, some of the negative characterizations of boys and men are true to life. I am not claiming that boys and men are without fault. Not by any stretch of the imagination. I am, however, casting light upon the terribly deficient models of masculinity and appropriate masculine behavior that have been foisted upon us by the entertainment industrial complex from the late 1980s onward.

My friends, the bar is set so very low. We are programming toxic masculinity instead of *divine masculinity.*

Wake up. Take the helm of your own mind. Come to favor personal accountability, individual responsibility, and having your feet held to the fire to ensure the gift of quick learning from mistakes, vowing never to repeat such mistakes again.

Learn the seven powerful lessons for raising healthy boys and mending broken men and live out those lessons in your way of being.

As you move forward on your path of self-refinement, know that you are not what the media portrays you to be. Unplug from such deleterious platforms. They are only serving to stultify your intellectual, physical, and spiritual growth. Know the proverbs of masculinity are almost universally, overwhelmingly negative and laced with a malevolent snarky undertone.

That characterization of boys and men in the media does not have to be applicable to you. Not at all. You are no goof. See the social constructions hyperbolizing and amplifying the gnarly toxic types of masculinity. Be the opposite.

Don't be a dope. Identify the toxic programming correlated with unhealthy boys and men. Then, defy such programming.

The most rebellious thing you can possibly do in a perniciously cruel world that is all too ready to scapegoat you as toxically masculine for its very own shortcomings is to rise above said toxicity, conducting oneself beyond reproach. Transmute yourself into the bona fide, indubitable embodiment of the divinely masculine.

It is now on you, my friends. You are each now responsible for saving your own lives. Or not. Need motivation? Let us turn our attention to the little-known, yet very real, barbarous statistics regarding boys and men in the United States of America today.

Statistics Regarding Men & Boys

Quite ominous indeed are statistics regarding boys and men in the West these days. Let us start with mass incarceration.

Did you know that the United States incarcerates more human beings than any other industrialized nation?

Check this out. There are nearly eight billion people riding this blue sphere called Earth, hurtling through the universe at a whopping 67,000 miles per hour.

Of those nearly eight billion people, a little over 331 million actually live in the United States of America. In fact, America constitutes less than five percent of the overall world population. In other words, if there were only one hundred people living on the entire planet, only five of those people would be living in America. Ninety-five of those individuals would be living elsewhere!

With that perspective in mind, take notice that in the present day, more than 22% of the global worldwide prison population is confined within the United States. So, framing it a bit differently, if there were only one hundred prisoners in the entire world, then twenty-two of those prisoners would be confined in America. Now that is the very definition of disproportionate.

In short, America likes to lock people up. Furthermore, it is boys and men who account for more than 90% of the nation's overall incarcerated population. Statistically speaking, if you are a boy or man in the West today, you have a "lock-up target" on your back. Boys and men are over eight times more likely than girls and women to get sent "up the river" to do a prison stint in this lifetime.

What is the lesson for boys and men here? Well, numero uno, if you are a boy or a man living in America, recognize the idea that the societal structure that you have found yourself in has little or no problem whatsoever with the notion of locking you up. They won't even bat an eye.

Being born with a penis can lead to a perilous prison experience for the unwitting young man or older adult man caught unaware of the seven fatherly lessons for raising healthy boys and mending broken men.

You do not have to be such a statistic. Liberate yourself. Create a different path. Develop a definite life purpose in the overall context of your life mission for yourself. Steer clear of the prison industrial complex (PIC). It has a propensity to create frequent flyers. You can do little or nothing confined in a detention center or prison cell.

Make the "noun choices" that will keep you out of the penal colonies for good. What is a "noun choice"? Let me elaborate: Nouns are *people*, *places*, and *things*. So, *who* are you hanging out with and why? *Where* are you going with those people? *What* things are you doing with those people once you get there?

Think about your future and what you really want to create, manifest, achieve, and accomplish in this lifetime.

Are the nouns – the people, the places, and the things – in your life currently going to lead you to jail or prison? If so, consider immersing yourself in new nouns.

Getting locked up is a very real possibility for many boys and men living in the United States. Do not be so hubristic to delude yourself. It can happen to you. As a boy or man living in America today, if you don't get locked up that may just be because you have been murdered.

According to the 2018 Uniform Crime Report from the F.B.I., of the 16,335 U.S. murder offenders, 10,639 were identified as male perpetrators. Only 1,511 of the homicidal offenders were identified as female. The remaining 4,572 murder offenders were of unknown gender.

Needless to say, it is most likely, given the preponderance of evidence we have seen introduced thus far, that the lion's share of the unknown gender category of homicide offenders is probably constituted of boys and men as well.

Without question, boys and men commit the vast majority of homicides in the United States. No shock. Who are these boys and men most likely to murder? Easy: other boys and men.

According to the 2018 F.B.I. Uniform Crime Report, of the 14,393 identified murder victims in the United States,11,096 of them were boys and men. Boys and men killing other boys and men, needlessly.

Of the homicide victims that year, 3,268 were identified as female, and twenty-nine of them were unknown. I can only imagine how that could happen. Bloodcurdling, no doubt.

Moreover, when it comes to "death by law enforcement officers," 992 human souls were shot to death in 2018. Of that number, 939 of them were boys and men.

Yet, after being fed toxic, processed "CRAP Frankenfoods" from the time of conception onward, nursed by PlayStations and Xboxes, coddled by inept parents and guardians, and left bereft of critical thinking skills by a broken-down public educational system, what can we really expect of this wayward lot of Technological Enfeeblement Syndrome (TES) suffering hooligans? Is this *Lord of the Flies* 2.0?

Unquestionably, the recent rash of gun-related mass casualties – as well as the horrific homicide levels – which have been a scourge on America's inner cities now for decades are a manifestation of the pernicious programming of boys and men. Times are tough for boys and men today. Times are ripe for change as well. As the 1960s folk artist, Bob Dylan, sang, "Times they are a-changin'." I definitely believe them to be.

Times They Are A-Changin'

Thank goodness times have changed. The way we treat women now is vastly different when juxtaposed with how they've been treated over the last hundred years. The ratification of the 19th Amendment granted women full, equal suffrage in the United States in 1920; however, many women were still discouraged from voting, especially in the rural south, until the late sixties. My own mother experienced some of these voter suppression tactics firsthand and also experienced gender discrimination when it came time to apply to colleges. She was not accepted into her first college choice, the University of Virginia, simply because, in that day and age, only men were deemed worthy enough to attend Thomas Jefferson's prestigious, masculine bastion of architectural design and development.

Instead, she and other female students were afforded separate and entirely unequal university accommodations, so she attended Mary Washington College (now Mary Washington University) in the nearby city of Fredericksburg, Virginia instead.

So tell me, why then do the antiquated proverbs of masculinity live on in our daily collective speech?

Given the new social realities of this alphabet soup identity age, shouldn't the very proverbs of masculinity themselves now be placed under microscopic scrutiny?

Such proverbs are inherently sexist toward boys and men.

It is now high time that society comes to terms with the notion that the very manner in which we have been programming our boys and men has failed in a miserable fashion, giving way to the notion that new approaches are needed now and going forward. Multitudes of examples abound in the nature of today's television programming.

Compare today's television programming, which consists of five thousand channels with no real substance, with the three or four television channels that were piped into houses in the West in the 1970s and early 1980s.

Bear in mind that the television used to go off at night, in the wee hours of the morning, after the playing of the national anthem, then returned to live broadcast the following morning, with the sunrise of a new day.

Another distinction is that television programming used to be somewhat educational in the early days of my childhood. Evening programing at that time featured the likes of Napoleon Hill and Earl Nightingale, imparting timeless wisdom through the discussion of life-success strategies.

Then, of course, there was the massive amount of knowledge conveyed through cartoon public service educational campaigns (e.g. *Schoolhouse Rock!*). Where and why did those types of educational television campaigns go by the wayside? Can we get them back? They are sorely needed today!

Schoolhouse Rock! provided an educative function that promoted a better understanding of governmental processes and the rights and responsibilities of active citizenship. Today's intellectually stultifying programming is a horribly debilitating waste of time. Moreover, contemporary programming largely consists of poor examples of living a joyous and liberated life. Unplug. Awaken.

Your time here on Earth is precious. Do not waste any more of your valuable energies on the frivolous and ultimately ephemeral short-lived, so-called pleasures of the unconscious mass-consumption life. People worry about pleasing multitudes of morons, going to and fro, never questioning the inculcative programming that has left them so enfeebled. Nike Air Jordans are simply just not worth the cost of shooting each other, folks.

Know now that you are responsible for your own life planning. Conduct your own resilience training. This life you are living is not a test run, my friends. This life is the real deal. Treat it as such.

You must awaken now or risk finding yourself looking back decades later, treading water in a sea of child support, drowning in credit card debt, living in your mom's basement if you are fortunate – living in a van down by the river if you aren't – pontificating about how the team would have won State decades ago if only your coach had put you in the game. Don't be that guy.

If you already are that guy, read this book cover to cover. Begin to undertake the liberative exercises toward self-refinement contained herein. Admit, and really know for real, that you simply *don't know what you don't know*. That is the starting point for all of us on the path of awakening spirituality. Seek to know. Everyone already knows that you don't know. Take sage advice, perhaps for the first time in your life.

I give you the assurance that it is never too late for any of us to begin walking the path of spiritual awakening. Go ahead now and turn off the idiot box television for good. Take your video game system to the mall. Sell it at that smelly little game store. Break your screen addiction to your phone. Use it as a tool, as a phone. Set aside the myriad of distractions, addictions, and old ways of being, as they are no longer serving your new walk along the path of the masculine divine.

Demystifying Divine Masculinity

The way of the divine masculine is a journey, bringing back information and lessons to bequeath to the world upon your return, culminating in the presentation of your gift to the world, my friends. Being an ardent reader of the work of Joseph Campbell, I consider it to be quite apropos to begin this teaching with an examination of masculinity, as seen through the lens of ancient mythological tale.

Going back to Hellenistic times in ancient Greece, the great poet Homer wrote his renowned epic titled *The Odyssey*. Homer's *Odyssey* is a recollection of a strange, exciting, and adventure-filled journey undertaken by the primary protagonist, Odysseus.

Although *The Odyssey* is told as an actual physical journey, undertaken in the real world in real time, I suspect there is hidden meaning behind the tale. Important spiritual lessons are often embedded within allegories. Perhaps Homer was really describing the notion of an internal journey, of a spiritual awakening, transpiring within one's own mind, body, and soul, allegorized through the adventures of Odysseus. For the purpose of interpretation, let us take that to be the case.

At one point on Odysseus' journey, our protagonist enters treacherous, siren-infested waters. Sirens are land-dwelling mythological creatures that are half bird, half lady. They're not to be confused with their cousins from the sea – mermaids – that are half fish, half human. Sirens use songs, just like mermaids do, to lure sailors to shipwreck on rocky coasts or jump overboard to be drowned in the sea. These magical siren songs are so powerful that men are unable to resist them; they either end up as dinner for these demonic bird ladies after they wreck or as shark feed while they sink to the ocean floor.

Odysseus knew how dangerous sirens were and ordered all of his men to plug their ears with beeswax to avoid being lured to their deaths, but he had his crew tie him to the mast - beeswaxless - so that he could still hear their songs without endangering his safety nor that of his crew's.

We all know how enrapturing feminine energies can be. You *must* tie yourself to the mast, just like Odysseus did, in your interactions with them to avoid the possibility of becoming overwhelmed. Do not be put off by the tumultuous nature of the feminine. Finding yourself lost in the torrent that is the essence of divine femininity is part of the allure and magic of life.

Stay your course. Run your race. See the divine feminine in all its divinely feminine glory. From your own inner Buddhist perspective, seek non-reaction and non-attachment. Observe the writhing world as you are grounded, tied securely to the mast. Protect yourself from the enchanting siren call, and remain in all ways steady on your path. Take the author of *The Art of War,* Sun Tzu's, advice: "If you know the enemy and know yourself, you need not fear the result of a hundred battles."

First and foremost, take note to know yourself. If you do not know yourself, it becomes impossible to perceive other human beings, whether they be friends or foes, with any real accuracy of understanding.

Hence, begin along the path of internal, introspective adventure. Human consciousness and the mind, body, and soul connection are the last unexplored continent on this three-dimensional plane. Adventure awaits you. Get to work.

Know you are a burgeoning human being. Learn to balance your masculine and feminine energies within your own body, supercharging your ability to manifest greatness, positivity, and light in this lifetime while bearing down healing radiance both upon yourself and the world around you. The time is now. Your challenge is to awaken spiritually in a high-tech era with little to no understanding of the path of human enlightenment.

Yep, these are indeed tough times for self-reflection, self-refinement, and self-realization.

Who has time to go inward and generate the self-healing work needed to evolve spiritually in this lifetime? These are tumultuous times, folks. Myriad digital distractions abound. Free speech is on the ropes. Contention, argumentation, and, most notably, righteous indignation have become ubiquitously pervasive in this contemporary, naysaying society. Fear looms large, casting its shadows of low vibrational, toxic darkness into nearly every aspect of our twenty-first century, social media-driven information age of shallowness and abject stupidity.

Technology makes a great servant but a poor master. How many of you know the art of cartography? Few or none. Well, I bet all of you have heard of Google Maps. Case in point. We have become the servants of our technological addictions. We are going to need a pill for that one too, I suppose!

Look for a new pharmaceutical remedy for our screen addictions and the like. It should hit the shelves at onset of the roaring 2020s. It is a cure-all for Technological Enfeeblement Syndrome *(TES)* named *GetOffYourButtAndDoSomethingGreat.* Ask your doctor if you may be suffering from TES and if *GetOffYourButtAndDoSomethingGreat* may be right for you.

This will be our reality soon, my friends. With all the instantaneous information availability in this brave, new 5G world, people are considerably more enfeebled today and considerably less resilient than ever. Jeepers creepers. Golly gee. People, what the heck is really going on here?

Physically, childhood and adult obesity rates in America are at stratospheric levels. An honest conversation about the toxicity of the highly acidic and largely processed CRAP Frankenfoods that have been introduced into our society as a cancerous Trojan horse is long overdue. Obesity is a national security crisis.

Intellectually, the United States is greatly lagging behind other industrialized nations in the arena of academic achievement. This is simply unacceptable. There is no good reason why kids in America are not in the top tier of each and every international academic area of measurement and testing. Our states, local community governmental jurisdictions, and parents and guardians must all do better.

It is high time to have a candid conversation about empowering a new sort of public school curriculum geared towards healthy and balanced living as well as towards the ultimate goal of cultivating critical thinking skills, all while emphasizing personal accountability and enhanced self-reliance.

Spiritually, we in the West are in rough shape. Darkness continues to close in upon us, feeding mercilessly upon the oblivious masses. The suicide rate in the U.S. continues to climb, now nearing up to 47,000 suicide deaths annually. The opioid and fentanyl crises, accompanied by other drug overdoses, claimed the lives of over 70,000 souls in the United States in the year 2017 alone. There is an abundance of malaise and darkness to go around. You don't have to look far to find it either.

The aforementioned physical, intellectual, and spiritual limitations and challenges constitute the environmental backdrop from a societal perspective at the time of this writing. There is an uphill trudge ahead if we are to pull ourselves from the abyss. We can climb out of Hell.

We must come to a more nuanced and spiritually advanced understanding of who we are as human beings. We have been afforded the great opportunity, the gift, of experiencing and lesson-learning within this lifetime. In a great sense of the word, all of us on Earth at this time are akin to lottery winners. We are truly blessed to be having this life experience, my friends. Yet, so few people truly get it.

People today are so inherently divided within themselves that they are manifesting very real and deleteriously consequential divisions between men and women, boys and girls. This has been going on for a while now. Remember the hyped up tennis match of 1973 played between Bobby Riggs and Margaret Court at the height of the women's liberation movement? The match never ended, apparently.

Today politicians exacerbate and amplify the differences between men and women, boys and girls, for one reason and one reason only: Power. Yet, deep down in that still small place within our hearts, we all know that we have been collectively hoodwinked. Let us examine the facts of your own conception.

Your mom's egg was fertilized by your dad's sperm unless you were conceived in a test tube. All human beings, including those conceived in a test tube, are of both masculine and feminine creative genesis. That is irreducible. It is axiomatic, a truth irrespective of how you identify along any socially-constructed gender continuum, no matter what your pronouns are or how you feel about the matter.

The very foundation of existence is based in the symbiotic dance of the divinely masculine and the divinely feminine energetic polarities.

Think of an electrical current. It has negative and positive polarities. When the two converge, there is a spark. That, my friends, is indeed the synergistic arc of attraction. The ancients knew the dualistic dance of the divine masculine and the divine feminine quite well. Quite well indeed.

In the ancient Hindu culture, human beings are envisaged as a divinely masculine entity (Shiva) morphed with a divinely feminine one (Shakti). Shakti and Shiva's conjoinment represents duality in unity.

The dance of Shakti and Shiva serves to characterize the arc of attraction – of negative and positive polarities whirling around down to even subatomic levels and within the very cells comprising each of our own bodies.

We human beings, all of us, are literally duality in motion. Both masculine and feminine energies reside within each of us. The divinely masculine man sees through the illusion of separateness. Self-aware, he balances the dance of the dualistic Shiva-Shakti cosmic energies within the very fiber of his existential, energetic being.

Yet, in this contemporary age of high technology and concomitant low spiritual understanding, the deck is really stacked against boys and men aspiring to awaken spiritually in this lifetime. Becoming liberated from the shackles of fear is an uphill battle indeed, my friends, but it's one you must fight!

If it is greatness you seek, look inward. Do not look outside yourself for validation, encouragement, monetary support, trustworthy information, or any real assistance whatsoever. Chances are, you won't find any. Walking the path of awakening to liberation and greatness in this lifetime demands you rely upon your own hands. What you seek is not outside of you.

You are the Holy Grail. The treasure you seek is within. The keys to freedom, joy, and immense abundance are all inside of you right here, right now. Realize it. Up to this point in your life, you have been inculcated and programmed to look to the outside expert to tell you what to do, how to do it, when, why, and where.

How has looking for the expert outside of you worked out for you so far? How has it worked out for your parents, siblings, friends, or colleagues? Bad news for some of you: truth be told, it hasn't. Do not delude yourself. Know now that the only way out is through. If it is liberation you seek in this lifetime, then you must earnestly commence with the self-refinement work, posthaste.

There is a roadmap for your work ahead that takes form in seven powerful fatherly lessons for raising healthy boys and healing broken men. You will know the divinely masculine boy or man when you meet him. The divinely masculine boy or man knows, and lives by, the following seven powerful fatherly lessons for this dispensation.

The Seven Powerful Fatherly Lessons
for Raising Healthy Boys & Healing Broken Men

1. **Sexuality is Sacred**
   - Demonstrate appropiate sexual behaviors at all times
   - Vet partners
   - Know the costs of fathering a child
2. **You Are What You Eat**
   - 75% of boys and men are overweight or obese
   - Eat sunlight foods
   - You are responsible for your own health
3. **Learn to Sow**
   - Sow, then reap
   - Depend on your own hands
   - Cultivate arete in all areas of your life
4. **Play with Heart**
   - Diligence is the great equalizer
   - Do not settle for mediocre
   - True joy results from great accomplishment
5. **Serve or Disengage**
   - Make use of strategic taciturnity
   - Never threaten anyone for any reason
   - Beware your digital footprint
6. **Covet Self Understanding**
   - Go inward
   - Learn to trust your gut
   - Seek self-realization
7. **Strength Needs No Introduction**
   - Pursue peace through strength
   - Never become violent with anyone for any reason (except in self-defense)
   - Serve and empower others as the way of strength

Lesson One: Sexuality is Sacred

We are not bulls in a cow pasture, gentlemen. The first of the seven powerful, fatherly lessons provides insight into the sacredness of masculine sexuality.

Emphasis is placed upon the extreme importance of vetting sexual partners, especially in light of today's economic and political environments. Mastering one's sexual urges is the starting point on this path. Self-discipline is key. Establish sexual dominion over thyself. Then, play the tape all the way through the decision-making exercise that is presented at the lesson's end.

Lesson Two: You Are What You Eat

Knowing that you are what you eat, both literally and figuratively, and the ability to move forward on that actionable intelligence is the focus of Lesson Two. According to the United States Department of Health and Human Services, almost three out of four men are overweight or obese. Boys are not far behind.

We in America today are gluttonizing ourselves and our progeny, consuming way too many Carbonated-Caffeinated drinks, Refined sugars, Acidic, and Processed foods (CRAP Frankenfoods). Stop feeding yourself, and your kids, CRAP Frankenfoods immediately.

This second step on the path involves mastering the tyranny of the taste buds. Gluttony is a big challenge for the majority of boys and men today. Primarily plant-based eating suggestions will be provided in the lesson. To grease the skids on effort to begin eating sunlight foods instead of darkness, the second lesson concludes with the exercise: Eat Sunlight Foods (Not CRAP Frankenfood).

Lesson Three: Learn to Sow

The third lesson on the path towards divine masculinity is reflective of Ralph Waldo Emerson's famous essay entitled, "On Self-Reliance." Learn to depend on your own hands. Learn to sow.

All too often these days, people just want something for nothing. This is an entitled age full of coddled babies. I am referring to the adults. The younger generations are far worse. Technological Enfeeblement Syndrome is at epidemic levels. Human beings have become confused by the reality of today. Freedom can never be found drinking at the government trough, or worse yet, buying from the company store. It is up to you to save your own lives, my friends. Lesson Three concludes with a time management exercise.

Lesson Four: Play with Heart

Lesson Four involves diligence. Your stick-to-itiveness. When you hear an announcer calling a football game say that the player "has heart," you know what that means. It means that the player has been diligent. Going an extra mile to make something magical happen on the playing field. Do that in life, creating opportunities for both yourself and for those around you.

Yet, be judicious when regarding whom you serve. Do not waste your valuable life force energies coming to the aid of those who are not deserving of your gifts. Your time is valuable. Do not waste it. Stop throwing pearls to the swine. It is a waste of time. Lesson Four concludes with the Breaking of Screen Addiction exercise.

Lesson Five: Serve or Disengage

The fifth lesson is to serve or disengage. Simply put, if you cannot be of service, then walk away. Disengage. That is your primary rule going forward for all human interactions. Live to fight another day. Without spilling one ounce of your precious energy. No sir. Not on those unworthy of your gifts.

Lesson Five concludes with the ever-so-powerful Non-reaction, Non-attachment, Just Walk Away exercise. That one will come in handy for you in the future. Bank on it.

Lesson Six: Covet Self-Realization

Lesson Six provides the stern and serious admonition to stop looking for the external expert. Cultivating your critical thinking skills and intuitive inner guidance is instead a much more sustainable path for you going forward, my friends.

Critical thinking, conjoined with the refinement of your visceral gut-level intuitive abilities, enables you to navigate this life with ease. Be like water. You should aim to effortlessly flow through both career and personal situations, unimpacted by the chaos out and about. You are centered, grounded in the foundation of knowing who you are, what you are doing, and why.

The sixth lesson culminates with the bequeathment of the Cultivating Arete in All Areas of Your Life exercise.

Lesson Seven: Strength Needs No Introduction

The seventh lesson on the path of transformation into the divinely masculine is to rise above prideful, ego-based needs for external validation. See your own insecure pretentiousness alongside and coupled with your own hubristic boasting and backbiting. Don't be so boisterous. Loquacity is vexatious. Superman does not need to announce that he has arrived at the fight. People know when he does. Similarly, the focus of lesson seven is that strength needs no introduction.

You will reach the top of your game after you sow your skills and achieve mastery. The recognition will come. Yet, do not seek recognition in life. Create value. Create abundance. Cultivate *arete* (Greek for excellence) in all areas of your life, and the rest will play out as it should.

You will be surprised how many accolades will arrive on your doorstep when you begin to walk the path of divinely masculine arete. The final lesson concludes with elaboration and future shock speculation on the challenges for divine masculinity on the near horizon in the age of toxic, Orwellian tribalism.

The Personal Strengths, Weaknesses, Opportunities, and Threats (SWOT) Analysis exercise can also be found at the lesson's end.

Go inward. Do the work. Exit the matrix. This book's conclusion provides a foolproof plan for immediate, personal, and strategic life planning for your self-reinvention.

Start today, knowing that the only way out is through. There are no shortcuts, my friends. In video game parlance, you need to level up.

Now onward to Lesson One: Sexuality is Sacred.

Lesson One

Sexuality Is Sacred

Sacred Versus Secular Sexuality

The divinely masculine boy or man has taken control of his mind, body, and spirit. The scorching hot flames of lascivious desire do not hold sway over him. Nothing overtakes his rational and intuitive functions. The divinely masculine boy or man is libidinously grounded, offering the utmost respect to the divine masculine, as well as the divine feminine, at all times. No matter the circumstance, he remains steady on his path.

To maintain such elevated reverence, the divinely masculine boy or man must learn to envisage sex and sexuality as being both sacred and sanctified. No less.

Sacred in the sense that intimate relations exist in the context of a love-based, consensual relationship built on trust, mutual understanding, and respect. Sanctified in the sense that the acts of intimacy should be pure, free from coercion, manipulation, and shyster sexual gamesmanship. Honoring commitments of fidelity within the context of relationship intimacy, the divinely masculine boy or man does not manipulate others for his own emotional, spiritual, or physical satisfaction. He is not that emotionally or physically needy.

In like manner, nor does he allow for the manipulation of his own precious spiritual human bodily vessel, by self-serving nefarious ends of others.

He sets healthy boundaries, aware of energetic vampires. He is nobody's victim.

The divinely masculine male takes both responsibility and accountability for his words, actions, and deeds. He is not readily or widely available. Vetting those within his circle of trust is standard operating procedure. All people, including his potential platonic partners, friends, and colleagues are examined with an eagle eye of scrutiny to weigh their worthiness to be in receipt of his time, gifts, and affection.

Potential romantic partners are held to an even higher standard. Much more education is needed for boys and men in this department, for sure. Your choice of romantic partner or spouse can literally make or break you.

In the absolute entirety of a man's life and existence, nothing has the unbridled potential to catalyze greater levels of blissful joy or hellish misery with more force, regularity, and certainty than the proper usage, or the freewheeling misuse, of one's sexual energies.

This information, regarding the sacredness and sanctity of sex and sexuality, is largely unknown. In fact, it is lost upon the masses. Indeed, the information being presented here is actually quite rare. Take it in.

Wake up. Do not let your libido pull you to and fro as you tag along for the ride. You don't have to be your libido's unwitting accomplice, marching ever faster toward your own financial ruin, or even worse, criminal prosecution. Can you say "incarceration"? Wake up.

No longer do you have to acquiesce and ride shotgun, as the victimized, nitwitted sidekick, while your hairbrained, libidinous urges impulsively handle the navigation. No.

Instead, you will now elect to proactively take the helm of your own mind, body, and spirit. Your thoughts, words, and behaviors are your responsibility. Own them instead of letting them own you.

This first lesson focuses upon both the recognition and the meditative regulation of the red sexual exergies swirling and swooshing around the groin area within you. Learn to recognize what is going on with the sexual energies within your own body. Learn to regulate the intensity and frequency of said sexual energies within you. Get a grip!

Sexuality, from a normative perspective, should be considered, spoken of, and acted upon from a grounded position. A position of reverent respect. Seeing sexuality as sacred by nature. There are a multitude of life benefits conferred before a divinely masculine boy or man who understands that sexuality is sacred. If, and only if, he governs himself accordingly.

As boys, and men in the United States, most of your lives you have been, and not so subtly so, programmed to exclusively think about, talk about, and act upon sexuality from a highly secular understanding of the topic. In particular, boys and men are force-fed one rather large, inherently pernicious lie regarding the understanding of both sex and sexuality in the current age.

That aforementioned pernicious lie is that the accumulation of money, fame, and power grants one sexual license. Sexual license with impunity, no less. The first erroneous conceptual component of the secular understanding of sexuality is that money, fame, and power will gain you unlimited sexual attention, and subsequent silence afterward, from any number of incredibly attractive potential partners.

That particular axiomatic life assumption might have been all well and good for Sammy Davis Jr., Frank Sinatra, and the rest of the so-called "Rat Pack" artists in their 1950s heyday, but today, that dog simply don't hunt.

Needless to say, there is not much, or any at all, counterbalance teachings of the sacred nature of sexuality in popular culture these days. Often, rich, powerful, and famous men have not been able to take no for an answer in regard to their sexual expectations of their entourages, fans, and underlings.

Remember too that the "Rat Pack" existed well before the time of instantaneous information exchange, and global hyper-connectedness that we share today, with nearly eight billion others along for the ride on this blue spherical planet, too. Times have changed, gentlemen. Amend the rules you live by today. Govern yourselves accordingly.

Dear readers, right now, stop living for some future day when you will have all the money, power, and fame needed to bed down a harem of hotties. That is just not how society works today, my friends.

The #MeToo Movement has exposed many men who have taken advantage of their money, power, or fame. There are examples aplenty. Does anyone remember a news guy named Matt Lauer? Way too many of us whittle away our days fantasizing about a better life, with more money, more attractive partners, and all the trappings of the greener grass we think exists just over yonder.

Yet, very few of us are actually getting present right now, completing work requisite for the creation of life. Changes are on the horizon. Stop living in fantasy land virtual reality.

Change your perspective. Change your life. When you begin to see sexuality as a sacred force shared in a love-based relationship, you will find that you waste considerably less time chasing the always elusory sexual fantasy, the dream goose chase.

How many countless hours a week do boys and men spend buying drinks in local watering hole bars, swiping right on Tinder, or engaging in some other version of the secularization of sexuality game? How much more could those boys and men be achieving with their academic pursuits? With their careers? With their workouts? With their entrepreneurial activities?

Think of all you could be. If you became all you could be. What is possible from flipping the script on the programming?

The divine masculine is focused exclusively on the attainment of a man's definite life purpose in the overall context of his life mission. A divinely masculine man is unrelentingly determined in the pursuit of his definite life purpose and of cultivating the highest levels of arete which pervades every aspect of his being.

Time is valuable to the divine masculine. Frivolity on the whims of others is simply not in his wheelhouse. He is not readily available.

Therefore, time spent with the divine masculine is valuable for those who are worthy to walk in his radiance. Like a diamond, scarcity increases one's value.

The divinely masculine man sees sexuality as sacred because he has immense respect for himself, as well as his partner, and that respect is the foundation for healthy sexual attraction. Activity without drama. Free from any and all histrionics. The divinely masculine boy or man's name is nowhere to be found in the social media gossip columns.

The divinely masculine man does not focus on the pursuit of sexual partners; instead, he focuses upon what he is manifesting, creating, and bringing forth into the world. Bold new ideas and conceptualizations, revolutionizing the way that human beings think, talk, and behave in extraordinary ways. Ways that only his own specific, focused talent could have brought forth as a gift to this world.

Stop thinking about pursuing romantic partners. Right now. Turn it off for a bit. Stop the continuous sexual chase. Just stop.

Redirect that energy toward the pursuit of your definite life purpose in the overall context of your life mission.

Incredibly, you will soon find that potential partners, the high-quality type of potential partners you are truly seeking, are drawn to you like moths to a flame. Stop thinking about finding sexual partners.

Start creating the very best you that can possibly manifest on the Earth in this lifetime. You will be simply amazed by the results. In very short order indeed.

Energy is not destroyed. It can, however, be consciously redirected.

Self-mastery is at the heart of the essence of the divinely masculine. Walking the path of the divinely masculine does not require you to look over your shoulder. You won't lose any sleep at night over careless whispers. Along this path, there will be no need to justify the day's thoughts, words, or behaviors. You will rest easy, knowing you are not losing your integrity. Welcome the change.

You can reprogram your brain. Scientists call it *neuroplasticity*. The ancients knew about it some time ago. They called it alchemy. The directions are encoded upon our very DNA strains, and this knowledge is already within you. Literally and figuratively. The key to your own liberation is the raising of your vibrational frequency.

The starting point to walking the path of sacred sexuality, as practiced by the divinely masculine, is avoiding the porn trap.

Avoiding the Porn Trap

The following are the top three reasons you should avoid the porn trap altogether.

First and foremost, the over consumption of pornography often results in intimate partner disconnectedness. Ironically, the squandering misuse of a human body's energy never leads to any long-term happy ending.

Secondly, erectile dysfunction (ED) is strongly correlated with excessive pornographic consumption. No worries. The pharmaceutical industrial complex has made seeing a urologist online now easier than ever. From the comfort of your own home, your husky corpulence can be prescribed erectile dysfunction medications that will be shipped straight away to your door in highly discreet packaging. No inconvenient trips to the doctor's office. No uncomfortable interactions at the pharmacy. How commodious! Minimize your pornography screen. Maximize your medical doctor ED appointment screen.

In just a few short days, your medication, necessary to sustain your porn-addicted, companionless lifestyle, will arrive in your mailbox posthaste. Not for me, gents. I am disembarking that ship of fools. Do the same!

Tertiarily, pornographic consumption is stultifying spiritually. Think about it. By all reputable investigative journalistic accounts, there is wide-spread abuse and manipulation, and even reports of human trafficking, of drugged-out, new-faced, barely legal lassies by the pornographic industrial complex.

Then with each successive new moon, that latest crop of now-defiled flibbertigibbets are ushered out and summarily kicked to the curb for a new harvest of starry-eyed, Instagram-celebrity-wannabee sapheads. It is all quite shameful. Certainly not the spiritual train I want to be riding upon. Are you really onboard with all that?

Without question, the consumption of pornography alters a boy or man's sexual taste. Unequivocally, the consumption of pornographic programming is decidedly damaging to one's relationships, sex life, and sexual fitness overall. Healthy love-based conjugal relations are rarely portrayed in pornographic films. Pornography is a very poor source of sex education indeed for boys and men today.

In fact, in the real world, if you attempted to act out a pornographic movie plot, you would, in all likelihood, be summarily fired, sued, and possibly criminally charged with lewd and lascivious behavior, sexual misconduct, rape, or worse yet, all three. Pornography is indeed a poor source of sexual education regarding how to properly conduct yourself in the #MeToo era, my friends. Not surprisingly, intimacy often declines once one, or both, partners develop preference for virtual-world fetishization, networked tantalization, and wired fantasizing over actual real-world, romantic partner intimacy with another live, incarnate human body.

Interestingly, studies have linked the consumption of pornographic materials with loneliness. Wouldn't that make sense? Pornographic merriment, as a pastime, is often a solitary endeavor. Step back from all of this and consider how pornography is impacting your life today. There are action steps that you can take to overcome the debilitating impact of pornographic addiction. Chief among them: Stop watching porn.

Many reading this work are hopelessly addicted to pornography. Much like cigarettes, pornographic material consumption is the unseen public health crisis, of epidemic proportions, plaguing the United States today.

Rapid technological advancement, coupled with darn-near global internet access and connectedness, has catalyzed many great advantages for the evolution of human spirituality. Yet, the very same technologies are being misused today. Creating much suffering throughout the land.

Two short generations ago, my grandfather, Colonel Lloyd Earl Wills (who jumped on D-Day during the historic invasion of Normandy that really turned the tides of WWII in favor of the Allies), was given cigarettes, non-filtered cigarettes no less, in his sea rations.

We wouldn't dream today of allowing our young brave men and women in uniform to be issued cigarettes as part of a wholesome, nutritious, and complete military-approved meal.

I strongly suspect that somewhere, from a future vantage point, that we may collectively look back and wince, wondering why on Earth we made an insidious force, such as pornography, so readily available to poison what has now turned out to be multiple generations of boys and men. A poisoning that has led to so much unnecessary suffering.

We are beginning to see the same type of retrospective – a "what the heck were we doing?" – analysis being played out with the big pharmaceutical companies.

Take notice of the opioid crisis. The pornographic industrial complex does not leave feces-stained overdose victims dead, awaiting on stairwells for the arrival of weary paramedics.

The impact of pornographic addiction leaves scarred and wrecked toxic human beings to walk amongst us treating each other with the spiritual awareness, compassion, and empathy of a zombie from the *Walking Dead* television series.

Emotionally wrecked people wreck people emotionally. You can get off this hamster wheel, cold turkey. I highly suggest it.

You can accomplish this much heralded and nearly impossible Herculean achievement of pornographic consumption cessation much easier than you realize. Remember, at the outset of this process, that energy is not destroyed. Energy can, however, be redirected.

Therefore, do not set out to quit watching pornography. Set out to enhance your sex life as well as your sexual wellness and sexual fitness, reinventing and reinvigorating your love life. With that very intention set, *then* stop watching pornography cold turkey.

It is not like cigarettes. There is no Chantix or prescription pill, at least not to my knowledge, that will assist with the cravings associated with pornographic withdrawal. Forget all that.

Instead, redirect the energies that you were previously putting into the pursuit of pornographic consumption toward the new end of cultivating a more powerful, and mutually much more satisfying, intimate relationship with your current partner. Or, if you are currently single, or sexually inactive, that is actually great as well.

Take this valuable opportunity to recreate yourself sexually. There is nothing wrong with being single. Abstinence is not weird. It is actually a form of energetic self-protection and psychic self-defense in a day when such protections are much needed.

You do not have to go to the prom. Or, to your twentieth high school class reunion for that matter. That is all ego. It is far more important to pursue your definite life purpose, in the overall context of your life mission, with a single-minded determination. Work on yourself first. Achieving the goals set forth for yourself prior to undertaking a serious relationship and or familial commitments is always a boy or man's best bet. Relationships are both time consuming and fiscally draining. Enter them wisely.

It is far better to begin a serious relationship, and to take on with seriousness the roles and responsibilities of parenthood in particular, once you have achieved your own educational and career goals.

Relationships tend to go better when you already have your sea legs beneath you. Get stable emotionally, financially, and spiritually first and foremost, my friends. Before that time, what do you really have to offer another human being? Aside from your fear-based neediness? What do you really bring to the relationship table, other than your appetite? If you are to be truly of service to both yourself, as well as to your potential partner, go in solid from the get-go.

Any relationship built on the shifting sands of fear, economic necessity and hardship, or any other rendition of fear-based insecurity and loneliness will most certainly not stand the test of time. When you think you are really ready for an intimate sexual relationship, strongly consider what you are seeking and why.

What do you really want from a fulfilling, and mutually beneficial, sexual relationship with a well-vetted partner whom you can trust absolutely? Protect yourself these days, gentlemen.

The key here is to enter only into romantic relationships with a partner who has as much to lose as you do. Or more.

Definiteness of purpose is the first step to making life changes and to the manifestation of the life on the horizon that you really want to create for yourself. Know what you are seeking in all areas of your life, including relationships, gentlemen.

Begin by setting healthy boundaries in your relationships. Anyone who is to be an occupant, within your inner circle of trust, must be seriously vetted. Romantic relationships are no exception.

Relationships & Vetting

Let us get it straight from the get-go that your first, and primary, most consequential and valued relationship should be with yourself. "The greatest love of all is easy to achieve. Learning to love yourself. That is the greatest love of all" (Whitney Houston, 1985). The identification and pursuit of your definite life purpose in the context of your overall life mission must come first in this lifetime, my friends.

Stop looking externally for your soulmate. Your twin-flame. Or, even your newest Tinder one-night stand and lust partner. Just stop. It is not working.

Prior to parceling out your precious time and energy toward a romantic partnership unwisely, it might turn out to be handy to get to know yourself. You will not find what you are truly seeking anywhere in the external. Nothing, outside of your own spiritual growth, will confer such a high-level gift.

You are the Holy Grail. Stop looking externally for a relationship to complete you. Approach any and all future relationships as a complete human being, seeking a synergistic connection with a well-vetted partner who has as much to lose or more than you do. Someone with a little skin in the game. A partner conducive to the pursuit of your definite life purpose, in the context of your overall life mission: your walk with the divinely masculine.

As simple as it sounds, that is the most heavily weighted criterion that the divinely masculine will need to use in the vetting of a potential romantic partner. Knowing beyond a shadow of a doubt that the potential partner you are considering will bring abundance to your life. Or, knowing oppositely that a prospective partner will serve to drain your precious life-force energy, leading you down the rabbit hole of self-induced mediocrity or, even harder to rebound back from, total life destruction. That too is really good information to know from the outset, before committing to a relationship with such a cretin.

If you don't take great pains to vet potential relationship partners, prior to jumping right in to going steady, prior to moving in, before getting engaged, or worse yet, ahead of eloping suddenly after dating for only two weeks, there may be high consequences on the horizon. They can rain down misery upon what used to be a life you valued. The life you once cherished. The very life you used to love and enjoy!

See through the smokescreens. People can say they love you to your face all day long. That is easy. Watch their actions. Listen attentively to the manner in which they talk about others. Much more about the personality of the potential romantic partner will be most certainly, and often shockingly, revealed when you tune in. Pay attention, my friends.

People are often quite adept at hiding who they really are, sometimes undiscovered for protracted periods of time, in the dating game, my friends.

So, when it comes to vetting potential relationship partners, just let go of any of those Pollyannaish ideas regarding the intrinsic benevolent nature of the hearts and minds uniting all human beings. Kumbaya. Those types of foundational assumptions simply will not serve you in the arena of dating. Work on your listening skills here.

Often, men hear what they want to hear after they have already become physically and emotionally addicted to a potential partner's wiles. Hear the reality. Not want you want to hear.

Listen to the way that the potential relationship partner, and her mother in particular, talk about the potential partner's father. Take notice. Tune in. This can all be quite revealing. Don't believe the hype.

Do not buy the story wholesale that your potential partner's father was a dead-beat dad, an abusive alcoholic, or any other form of nefarious character presented to you. That may all be true, of course. If you decide to pursue a relationship with that partner, prudence would lend to ensuring that the potential partner has undergone the type of self-work, healing, and forgiveness necessary to break the cycle of abuse. Take care that your relationship does not become a sequel to that abuse, as they so often do these days, as your life unravels because of your dysfunctional partner's paternal issues. Much of your happiness will come from what you did not get involved with in this lifetime, my friends.

I get it. There are some really horrible dads out there. That is for sure. Don't become one yourself, by the way. Yet, there are just as many horrible mothers out there, too. Often, people believe the narrative of the mother, most typically portraying the father in a highly negative light. It is best to avoid all this nonsense altogether. Listen to what your potential partner says early in the courtship to protect yourself from pitfalls just down the road.

It is a good rule of thumb to insert your name into the sentence whenever your potential partner mentions her father. Whatever the potential partner is saying about her father, she will most likely be saying about you when you split up. If you have kids with that partner, it can be an eighteen-year sentence of listening to that inane, amateur psychological gibberish.

The same rule of thumb generally goes for the potential partner's previous boyfriends. Insert your name in whatever the potential partner says about one of those lads. Know upfront that when the two of you break up, you will be the new case study in masculine toxicity. Beware of such emotional vampires.

This is serious business, gentlemen. The life decisions you make regarding sexuality have real-life consequences. Serious ones of the body-slamming variety. Real-life consequences that can ruin you financially, deplete your emotional capital, lead to court action and deposit in the local detention center, or worse yet, land you up the river, doing a stint in state prison. The list of pitfalls of the rampant misuse of one's sexual energy is long and not so distinguished. Let's start by examining the phenomenon of child support.

At the very surface level of reality, child support is a social safety net to ensure that the mother, who is usually awarded residential custody either *de facto* by family court order or *de jure* by default, and the children have sufficient income to survive once the father has been banished from the household. Often, public policies have the best intentions. You know what is said about the best intentions don't you? The road to Hell is paved with them.

The road to Hell, in this particular case, is paved with public policies that have provided monetary and tax return incentives, leading to the expulsion of the father from the residential domicile where the children are being raised.

In fact, child support is the manifestation of failed, socially-engineered, public policy projects that have left three generations – Gen X, Gen Y, and now, Gen Z – bereft of strong and compassionate, divinely masculine leadership and influence within the familial domicile during the crucial rearing years.

Society is paying an untold price for the poor public policy decision making on the part of many of our elected officials. The ones who have sought to further their corporate-funded political careers – lining their pocketbooks handsomely along the way – over true representation for and service to the American people. It is a damn shame.

Think about this before you consent to have children with anyone. It is a hostile world out there. Your best interests will not be in the forefront of your ex-partner's mind if the show ends poorly, gentlemen. No matter how well you think that you know that person.

The State will not be much nicer when you end up in family court, either. By the way, just so you know, family court is often not too friendly to the men who come before the hearing officers and judges.

Once child support orders are cast forth, not paying, even due to unemployment or unforeseen illness, can result in a man's driver's license being suspended. It is very hard to get to work or school, gentlemen, without a driver's license. Further inability to pay child support can and often does result in child support jail sentences. Imagine this scenario. Learn from the anecdotes in this book. Do not let this be you.

A guy I once knew was walking back to his mom's house where he was living post-divorce. His head hung low with an aura of pitiful sadness about his entire demeaner. His countenance was stone-face stoic.

The thought that this shouldn't be happening to him never occurred to him anymore. Nope. That thought left him around the sixth month of his jail sentence for not paying child support. The epiphany suddenly hit him one day while he was confined in the detention center.

He was not a victim. He had voluntarily given away his freedom. His monetary savings. His very dignity. His self-respect.

Allowing himself to be dragged down further and further into a highly toxic relationship with an emotionally, and often physically abusive, mega-toxic partner with whom he shared children.

As the light spring rain began to drizzle down upon his dress clothes and the soggy paperwork he had secured in an thin, clear jail trash bag tucked underneath his right arm, the man made the turn onto his mother's street. He had moved back into his childhood home to reset and reinvent his life.

No matter where you are currently, whether it be in the middle of a toxic relationship, a divorce, a child custody battle, or a child support modification hearing, know there is a light at the end of the tunnel.

The man walking home in our story did, in fact, regroup. He continued onward to lead a wonderful life, one of joy and service to others. He was able to unshackle himself from that toxic relationship.

Wake up before you find yourself in the soggy shoes of the guy above, walking home with a Herculean job of life reinvention ahead of him. It is far better to build an empire and keep it the first-time.

Just to be clear, emotions often run high in romantic relationships. This is especially true when there are children involved. At stake often, as children are used as financial pawns between warring family law attorneys.

See the warning signs for yourself and be proactive. Often, it is abundantly clear to everyone else around you that your relationship has spun out of control in terms of the frequency, and the severity, of the verbal, and sadly even physical, confrontations.

Some partners are like a narcotic. The relationship started great, and you got hooked. Now, the relationship has turned incredibly hostile and toxic. You find yourself in a quagmire, buried up to your neck, stuck inexorably in an environment making you sick emotionally, physically, and even spiritually.

Know the warning signs of a toxic relationship. Get out. A good man can rebuild his life, with more helpful people in his radius. If you decide definitively to leave a toxic relationship, be sure to make it a clean break. Take great means to avoid being accused of stalking or cyberstalking.

Do not orbit anyone's residence, or work area, once the break-up has ended. I don't care how much you hurt. The police will not care too much either, by the way.

I advise you to unfriend, and completely disconnect online, with ex-partners as well. Do not write anything online, or text anything to anyone for any reason, that could be interpreted as derogatory or hostile in any way toward your ex-partner.

Again, go for the clean break.

Whatever feels good to say, post, or text in the heat of your emotional throes, while writhing in heartbreak pain, lying in fetal position on the floor, will be used against you. By others as they poke fun at your misery online, or by the police as they investigate a report of stalking, cyberstalking, harassment, or worse.

Don't phone and fret. Cry, and get all of your emotional baggage out to the surface, for sure, just don't make social media posts or texts about the situation that may forever memorialize that horrible moment for all posterity!

As a general rule, leave as small of a digital footprint as possible, all the time. Pursue arete to the ends of the earth, yet do not attempt to go it alone. When you are emotionally, physically, or spiritually hurting and healing, reach out to a trusted mentor that will listen to you, guide you, and keep your situation from reaching the ears of others.

Often times, talking about these types of events, rather than acting inappropriately in a less-than-useful manner, will lead to a far-better ending spot. Both for you, as well as for the other people involved. Take the road less traveled.

No matter what happens, do not ever even consider committing suicide. Your life is precious, my friend. Do not throw away this tremendous opportunity to grow and evolve spiritually, right here right now on the Earth. Hell is no place to stop. Do the work to pull yourself out of there. You will be glad you did.

Yet, no matter how bad you feel or how hurt you might be, in such times of emotional upheaval, you must tighten up. Like Odysseus, tie yourself to the mast. The torrent of emotions, the rampages of violence, punching walls – not at all advised by those of us who have suffered multiple metacarpal breaks – and other damage done to ourselves in such unwieldly emotional states will all pass in due time. Time heals all wounds, my friends.

If you conduct yourself in a manner that is less than useful or inappropriate, or worse yet illegal, there will be consequences. With just one misstep, you will forever memorialize the horror of the absolute worst moment of your life. You will never be able to forget being fired or forced to resign from a place of employment. Or, worse, a criminal conviction based upon your inability to traverse the sea of the sirens. Know that you are completely responsible and accountable for all your thoughts, words, and actions. No matter the throes of the emotional battering that you are taking at the time, do not make such excuses. Refuse to play the victim.

Society has changed considerably since the time of my childhood in the 1970s. There is a hyper focus today on toxic masculinity. Sometimes, for good reason.

Wake up, guys. The days where I saw men slapping a waitress on the behind as they walked by the booth where I ate my kid-sized grilled cheese sandwich as he simultaneously referred to her as “little lady” are dead and gone. Thank goodness and for good reason!

What I witnessed as a boy was one hundred percent sexual harassment of the exceedingly overt variety, no doubt. Sexual harassment should be avoided at all costs.

Respect yourself as the divine masculine. Respect the divine feminine. No exceptions, guys. Adopt new rules to keep yourselves out of the frying pan!

Do not speak to a woman’s physicality at all, going forward. Commenting on a woman or a girl’s, figure, weight, breast size, or other physical characteristics, either to her face or behind her back, is unkind and usually leads to problems down the road for those making such comments.

Moreover, completely avoid falling into the habit of making undue sexual advances in inappropriate settings. Know that the time for being sexual is with a well-vetted partner, in whom you have the highest levels of trust.

If you are at school, college, or university, focus on your education, learning, and training. Sit in the front row. Avoid electronic distractions. Pay close attention to the instruction. See your education as being both a privilege and blessing.

Be thankful. There are many highly capable boys and men all over the globe who would relish the opportunity to undergo such training and education. The type of training and education that would bequeath enhanced opportunities and provide a better living for themselves as well as their progeny. Know, you are blessed with opportunities. Do not forsake them!

Take your educational and training opportunities seriously in this lifetime. Become the best student you can be. Strive to become the second teacher in the room. Becoming the second teacher in the room means that you, with great attention to detail, follow the directions of the instructor. Energetically, you push the entire class collective forward toward the achievement of the course learning objectives.

Do not think of your educational or training setting as being one big real-world, real-time Tinder account. Keep your professional life professional, and if you are currently in school full-time, you are a professional student for the time being. All your romantic relationships should be separate from your professional life. When you are at school or training, do not behave like a herd of male lemmings. Conduct yourself like a gentleman instead. Respect yourself and respect all others with your thoughts, words, and actions at all times.

For my working-age readers, the very same principle applies to the workplace environment. Nowadays, learning this lesson can be harder than ever in the real world. So, do yourself a favor and internalize this principle, right here and right now. Keep your professional life professional.

We all know it. Workplace romantic entanglements only serve to derail your career path in the long run. Yes, they may be fun and alluring. Especially in the beginning as your mental floss escapes to fantasy land.

But when things derail, as they so often do, would your workplace be the preferred location to air out all of your dirty, secular-relationship laundry? I think not.

These days, the workplace environment has morphed into a laboratory of social testing. An anthropological and sociological nightmare, wherein almost everyone is offended nearly all the time. All too often, people are nowadays offended by innocuous or even jocular ways of talking and ways of being. Tighten up here, my working-age guys. The traps are being set for you. Be careful as you traverse the minefields.

Beware. Be on guard. Keep your head on a swivel. Watch everything that you say and do in your workplace environment. Avoid even the appearance of sexual harassment impropriety. Imagine everything you say and do is being recorded. It just may be. Treat work colleagues as work colleagues. Pursue romantic relationships elsewhere. Or, pay the price. It is up to you.

Secular sexuality is omnipresent in the postmodern, twenty-first century world. It is the norm; yet, that doesn't mean it is not a pitfall for your life as a boy or a man trying to negotiate the waters of this tumultuous time of social upheaval.

Know before you engage in sexual activity with any partner that secular sexuality can be weaponized. It often is. Secular sexuality can be used as a sword by one's political or business adversaries, as well as ex-romantic partners. It can get nasty. Especially when there are children involved. Behaviors that are incentivized by the allure of windfall monetary gain have served to destroy the American familial unit. Much unhappiness for both men and women has been the result.

Wake up to the idea that you must govern yourself accordingly to ensure that you never have to experience the exceedingly negative consequences of your own poorly-thought-out secular sexual decision making.

Sexual harassment, sexual assault, and, worst of all, rape are *never* permissible under any circumstances. None whatsoever.

In addition to that, I will double down and go one further. You should take extreme pains to avoid even the appearance of impropriety when it comes to the overall treatment of your romantic partner. Remember too, that the appearance of impropriety, when it comes to the myriad transgressions of sacred sexuality, is often equally as reputationally deleterious as the actual act of doing something improper!

It is on *you*. Never allow yourself to fall prey to a partner who would kiss and tell, burning your career or political aspirations down the road.

Be wary of any partner who may extort you for money under threat. See the troubles ahead before they are actually on your path. Steer clear of that iceberg. Make navigational changes to the trajectory of your life. Tomorrow may just be too late.

The days of the free love 1960s are over, my friends. These are much more dangerous times. The furtherance of the evolution of secular sexuality's invasion into every nook, cranny, and corner of American life ironically has not resulted in enhanced sexual liberation for the masses. Not at all. Quite the opposite. We are all now walking on eggshells around each other!

Know the dangers of secular sexuality. Be advised of the consequences of debauchery. It is far better to know now, upfront. To avoid the traps, rather than looking back in tear-filled retrospect, wondering how in the heck all this happened to you while you bury your face in your hands, sobbing after you have lost your job, or worse yet, as you sit hunched over in the interrogation room of a police station.

Danger, Will Robinson. Know the dangerous rip tides of secular sexuality. Govern yourself accordingly. Armed with proper information prior to setting out on sexual conquests, you will be protected. Take on the shield. This is a serious caveat here, gentlemen. Take heed.

When secular sexuality has run amok in your thinking, words, and behaviors, it has the uncanny and unique power to catalyze unintended consequences in your life that you never even saw coming. Be warned. Consider walking the path of sacred sexuality as a much more fulfilling path, long term. When done right, your existence can be darn-near completely drama free! What type of price tag could we put on a drama-free existence? It is damn-near invaluable, my friends.

As you choose your own adventure in this lifetime, do yourself a huge favor and take great pains to remember this one thing:

No matter how much power, fame, fortune, or money that you accumulate, it is the way you treat others that matters. Karma is a female dog. Do not take on the vibration of the Incubus.

The Incubus Story

An Incubus is a male demon. One that preys sexually on sleeping feminine beings in their less-than-conscious, unwitting slumberous state, no less. The earliest mention of the Incubus mythology dates back to ancient Sumer, some twenty-five hundred years ago. So yeah, the idea has been around a little while.

Yet, it is the exact same story that we see with powerful men on Earth, today. Old wine in new bottles, so to speak.

The chief characteristic of the Incubus is the power differential. Sexual relations with the Incubus are never fully consensual as his victims are all asleep. Who are the Incubi of our present day? Well, we have seen a wide variety of masculine figures, from newsmen, to movie producers, A-list actors, and even some sports heroes fall from grace as of late. Have we not?

The allegations surrounding the fall-from-grace examples of toxic masculinity are serious. They should be taken as such. It is never ok to sexually harass, sexually assault, or rape another human being. For any reason. At any time. Period.

The divinely masculine should take great pains to avoid even the appearance of such improprieties. Be smart. Avoid school and workplace relationship entanglements. Be professional. Act as if you are always being recorded.

If you see some of the character flaws of the aforementioned fall-from-grace men in yourself, good work. There is still time to change. You may want to avoid running for public office, however, as that opens a whole new can of worms.

The first step in redirecting the energy behind less-than-useful, and often inappropriate, sexual misbehaviors is to recognize the patterns of our thinking, talking, and behaving. The less-than-fully conscious patterns that we have fallen into. Know when you are going on autopilot. Sad but true. We are often the last to know.

Become aware of what you are doing and determine why, through introspection and meditative advancement. Take the helm of your own mind. See the toxic world surrounding you. Be in it. Consciously. Yet, don't be of its suffering.

Awaken to your own inner wisdom and begin to allow your highest wisdom to heal you from within. Think of it like this.

Remember "garbage in/garbage out?" As long as you are putting garbage fuel in your system, you can expect garbage, in the form of thoughts, words, and actions, to come out.

Take the time to step back and think about the toxic foods that you are introducing to your body each and every day. Get rid of the carbonated and the caffeinated, gentlemen. It is time to clean up the fuel for your fire.

Upgrade, upgrade, upgrade.

Upgrade to a cleaner energy source for the provision of a rock-solid foundation upon which to build the life of your dreams, my friends. Pay close attention to what you are putting in your body.

You Are What You Eat Exercise 1: Carbonated & Caffeinated

As a small child in the 1970s Western world, my grandmother and my parents both had huge gardens in their respective backyards. Those two relatively small plots of land produced a virtual cornucopia of organic, non-GMO sunlight foods for my family to eat.

Fruits and vegetables from our own compost-fertilized backyards, that was the way of my childhood. How rare is that experience for the majority of Americans today!

People back then ate more sunlight foods. Sunlight foods contain the synergy of the earth, sun, air, and ether. #SunlightFoods. People, in those days, drank much more water as well. That was just what people did.

Soda pop was much more of a luxury item. Akin to eating a piece of cake on a special occasion. At that time, what we know now as convenience stores, (what I call 'the toxic sugar, killer tobacco, and lottery addiction outlets'), were actually very few and quite far between. Certainly not on every corner strip mall, as they are today.

Enter any convenience store in the United States. You will immediately see walls of coolers, containing sugary toxic sodas and energy drinks, marketed to kids, as well as a wide variety of cheap, just-as-sugary, toxic alcoholic beverages marketed to adults.

Sugary and toxic being lowest common denominator. The elephant in the room.

Both the sugary sodas and energy drinks, as well as the alcoholic beverages, are making people sick. Very sick. I don't care what your friends, teachers, relatives, role models, Instagram heroes and heroines do, say, think, or feel. They do not know that they do not know. Think for yourself. Convenience stores are gas-and-addiction stores. Begin to see things as they are.

Part of the challenge facing the high body mass index (BMI) boys and men of today is their relentless consumption of sodas, energy drinks, coffee, and other toxic, caffeinated beverages. It's a scourge of sugary destruction eviscerating the lives of so many.

If you really want to get lean and look and feel better than ever, you must pay the price of the rebel: initial discomfort. As the delirium of sugar withdrawal tests your will, your ego will do its damn-level best to get you side-tracked down the path of sugar consumption, again and again. If you fall off the horse, get back on. The cravings will go away. You can do this!

The first You Are What You Eat exercise calls for the immediate and everlasting cessation of the consumption of all carbonated and caffeinated beverages. That means all sodas, especially diet sodas with aspartame, coffee, caffeinated teas, and all of the so-called energy drinks. The ones that really only serve to drain your energy, leaving you hanging in a stupor after spiking your blood sugar.

Going forward, your sole source, mainstay provider for hydration and liquid refreshment should be water. Begin consuming water exclusively throughout each and every day.

Don't get me wrong, I understand that a soda is tasty. Have one once in a blue moon. I too enjoy a cola drink every once in a while. Instead, however, I opt for the cane sugar versions of cola that can be found at health food grocery stores, where I advise each of you to begin grocery shopping.

In Lesson Two, coming up, I will break down the nature of what I refer to as CRAP Frankenfoods, in great detail. CRAP Frankenfoods is an acronym for Carbonated/Caffeinated, Refined sugars, Acidic foods, and Processed foods. Here in Lesson One, you have already addressed the C and gotten into the CRAP in your life.

You control your current, your intensity, your frequency. Make sure you are always well hydrated. Drink water, without exception, throughout your day. In the evening, especially prior to bed, take a cup of decaffeinated hot tea, if you like. With local honey, from your particular region of the globe, as the only sweetener. No sugar.

The same way you do not need pornography to jumpstart your sex life, you do not need coffee, or other caffeinated drinks, to jumpstart your day. Learn to recognize and regulate the energetic flow within your own body.

As you prepare for your night's rest, consume the hot tea, giving thanks to the universal Creator for your day's protection and learned experiences. Just prior to bedtime, spend a few moments in reflection. Do this each evening.

Reflect back on what you did right, as well as what could have been improved upon, in the day gone by. Make self-corrections, vowing not to make those or similar mistakes ahead. Forgive yourself and all others. Rest. Begin again anew. Wake to perform the Five Tibetans in the morning.

Workout Exercise One: The Five Tibetans

Workout Exercise One focuses on The Five Tibetans. The Five Tibetans are an ancient set of exercises that I perform after my morning meditation. The Five Tibetan exercises are an energetically enlivening practice, one that is sure to get the juices flowing, setting your day on a path of arete.

Think about it. You sleep in a stationary position. Many of us work in sedentary, sitting careers. Long periods of stasis create what I refer to as energetic static pooling within the human body. This pooling of energy leads to disease.

Movement is life. Stasis is death. So, doesn't it make sense to invigorate your human body upon awakening, to prepare to have the best day possible? Unless you up and quit your job, you are going in to work, anyway. Why not make the work experience great for you, as well as for those in your radius? Wake up and invigorate.

Turn your phone off or at least mute the device. Put it out of view. No distractions, my friends. You are on a life-enhancing path of revolutionary emancipation. Pay attention to your mission of health, wealth, and happiness. You are worth it. Without further ado, let's get to doing the Five Tibetans.

12345

Stand upright for the First Tibetan. Bring your toes, heels, calves, and thighs together, lengthening the spinal highway, allowing for maximum nerve signal communication spanning heels to crown.

Bring your arms straight out to your sides, palms down. Pick one spot in front of you. Your *driste.* See that spot. Begin rotating clockwise, keeping your feet as close together as possible, in wobble fashion. As you increase speed, without losing control and breaking form, you rotate faster still, stimulating the energies in the lower half of the body. The base of the spine tingling, energy surging upward ascending the spinal highway.

Remember to stay in control during this first Tibetan. Don't overthink it. In fact, for you eggheads out there, completely forget about any notion of molecular physics, angular momentum, or gravity. *Feel* where you are, instead. Use your viscera. Your gut. Your inner knowing. Your breath.

Remember that it is far better to do fewer, controlled First Tibetan exercises instead of many sloppy ones. Take it slow. Work on form. Advanced practitioners should go for twenty-one repetitions. Those just learning, or reentering a Five Tibetan practice, take it easy. See what you have in the tank today. Rome wasn't built in a day!

The physical, emotional, and spiritual damage that you have endured in this lifetime did not happen in a singular day either. Directly at the completion of the First Tibetan, move to the ground in supine position, to begin the Second Tibetan.

Lie on your back, assuming the supine position, face up, to begin the Second Tibetan. Bring your toes, calves, and thighs together, with your hands pressing into the ground, palms down, arms by your side.

Inhale, raising the feet and head directly to the sky without moving your hips, lower back, or torso. Form the body into a J shape. Repeat twenty-one times for advanced students.

Those just starting out on the Five Tibetan path, do as many as you can without losing the form. Once again, you are far better off doing the Five Tibetans with great form as opposed to mediocre results that come from sloppy technique and practice. At the completion of the Second Tibetan, move straightaway to the Third Tibetan. You got this.

If you are breathing, you are living. If you are living, you can make a concerted effort to improve your health resilience. Cut the crap. Get to work. Come to your knees to begin the Third Tibetan. Knees pressing into the ground, heels connecting with your gluteus maximus. Sit straight up on your heels. Envision a tiny, silver thread attached to the very top of your crown, encouraging you gently to lengthen the lower back, middle back, and the neck through to the stratosphere.

Lengthen the spinal highway, from the divine at the base of the spine, through the bountiful, beautiful balance of the crown chakra. Place your hands in your jeans' back pockets or pretend to if you're not wearing jeans.

Squeeze an imaginary quarter between your shoulder blades, elbows getting acquainted with each other, moving in gently. Exercising tremendous self-care for the beginners, exhale, bringing your head up to see the ceiling, or the sky, above you.

Continue looking backward, from your kneeling knees and heels position, ever lengthening the spinal highway, so eventually, you see down well down the backdrop of whatever is physically behind you. See the wall or the sky behind you. Keep going back. More. See the floor or the ground behind you.

Go for twenty-one repetitions, if that is in your capacity today. Aim for fluidity of motion and right technique. Remember breathe. The exercises may be catching up with some of you right now.

No worries.

You will build your endurance. Concomitantly, you will heal your physical, spiritual, and emotional bodies. Onward now, my friend. We are nearly done! Right away, do not think about your phone or other smart device, move to the Fourth Tibetan. Get on it. Lean into it.

Come to a seated position, placing your hands palm down, alongside your buttocks. Press into the hands and feet simultaneously, raising your hip flexors up to the sky. Inhale, allowing your head to gracefully fall back as your knees, belly button, and collar bones fall into position, along one parallel, longitudinal line, along the surface of your body.

As always, go for twenty-one repetitions. If, and only if, you can do them with impeccable form. When you lose the breath, or the form, stop the asana. You will have the opportunity to redeem yourself tomorrow.

There is no graduation, folks. There is only continuous improvement. Regroup, clear your head, and move to Downward Facing Dog to begin the Fifth Tibetan.

Hands pressing into the ground in front of you and toes bear-hugging the rear of the mat, as your hips rise high to the sky, begin the Fifth Tibetan in Downward Facing Dog. Many of you may have done Downward Facing Dog in a local power yoga or gym yoga class. If not, no worries.

I practice twenty-one repetitions of each of the Five Tibetans every morning after my morning meditational exercise. I find the synergistic power of that coupling to be invigorative for my human bodily vessel. Kickstarting a strong steady current of energy from heels to crown. One that gets me through my morning. Usually, at the top of my game.

When you leave your home and head off to work balanced, it is a game changer.

It is really hard for the road-rage jerk, the micromanaging boss, the neurotic teacher, or the inept administrator to get under your skin when you are in a serene state of mind. No one has the ability to sandbag you into making an unforced error when you are balanced energetically. You are responsible for your words and actions in society.

Boys and men who fail to grasp this simple notion end up living collectively in jail detention centers and in prisons. Those are not bastions of hope for critical-thinking boys and men. Instead of following the groupthink herd, learn to think for yourself. Awaken. Do your morning meditation each day followed by your practice of the Five Tibetans. Freedom from the bondage of self, society, and suckerdom await. You are your most valuable asset. Start acting like it!

Practice the Five Tibetans each morning to generate ever-increasing levels of energy that will be stored within the human bodily vessel for usage throughout the upcoming day. If you cannot pull off the twenty-one repetitions for all of the Five Tibetans, remember to do what you can. It is far better to do some than none.

Work your way up to doing twenty-one repetitions for all Five Tibetans. Set goals. Attain them. Remember that energy is not destroyed. It can, however, be redirected. Without further ado, on to Meditation Exercise One: Red Grounding.

Meditation Exercise One: Red Grounding

The meditation exercises, located at the end of each chapter, are cumulative, meaning that they build upon one another. Pay close attention here in Exercise One, as it will serve as the foundation for Exercise Two, and so forth and so on.

Prior to the undertaking of Meditation Exercise One, Red Grounding, go to the piano, or the internet, and locate the intonation of the low C note. Internalize the low C note. Know it. You will need this Om frequency later in the meditation.

Begin Exercise One in a seated meditative position on the floor. Sitting upright in a chair will serve as well, if modification is needed. Each of the exercises in this book begins in a meditative, seated position on the floor. Sitting in a chair is always offered as a modification.

Spine straight, sit upright, and chin up now, close your eyes. Set the intention here. The intention to let go.

What happens when you pour new tea into a teacup that is already full to the rim? Well, the tea just spills over onto the saucer. The renowned martial artist and philosopher, Bruce Lee, says that to receive new tea – or new information – we must remove the old tea.

Think of this grounding exercise in a similar manner. Really let go, at least for a little while, of the churning circus of cacophonous thoughts running roughshod through your busy mind, like an endless cable news story loop. Begin to feel your sitting bones if you are on the floor. If you are seated in a chair, begin to feel the soles of your feet touching the floor beneath you.

Now that you are in a comfortable meditative position, you will begin this grounding exercise with a breath work warmup. This type of breath work is referred to as *pranayama breathing.*

Breathe in through your nose, inhaling for eleven seconds. As you exhale, count back down from eleven. Repeat this until you can count up and down from twelve. Then, thirteen. Continue onward until you can slowly inhale for a count of twenty-one. Then, slowly exhale for a count of twenty-one. By fifteen seconds, you may feel that you have reached your peak. Your limit. Meaning you cannot possibly inhale any more air into your alveoli. That is fine. That is where you are today. Work up to twenty-one.

When you have reached your peak for that day, acknowledge your effort. Set the intention to go forth to achieve one more second of inhalation / exhalation in your meditative practices the following day.

This is a practice, people. Yet, some of you may be still able to inhale/exhale beyond fifteen seconds.

If that is indeed the case, please feel free and go on with the inhalation/exhalation beginning grounding exercise. Inhale for sixteen. Exhale for sixteen. Inhale for seventeen. Exhale for seventeen.

Now, really bring attention, and awareness, to the area of your belly button. During each exhalation, pull the pit of your belly to your spine. Then, release as you inhale. Inhale for eighteen. Exhale for eighteen.

Paste the tongue to the roof of the mouth, consciously creating a circuit. With such completed circuitry, the energy rages up your spinal highway, through the tongue into the roof of the mouth, driving the energetic surges upward between your eyes and through your crown.

Inhale for nineteen. Exhale for nineteen. Bringing attention to the tingling sensation in your central forehead, inhale for twenty. Exhale for twenty. Really begin to feel the energy running through your entire human bodily vessel, as your body becomes highly oxygenated. Perhaps for the first time in a while.

Remember a few years back when hyperbaric oxygen chambers were all the rage? Well, in fact, they were onto something. A highly oxygenated human bodily vessel heals expeditiously. Yet, you really do not need an expensive oxygen chamber to get the job done.

Make use of your own internal technology. Once discovered within, it is amazingly nuanced.

Now, inhale for twenty-one and exhale for twenty-one. Give it all you got, here. Really focus on lung alveoli expansion in receipt of whole-body, oxygenated healing.

Good work! The endgame of this exercise is to keep pressing the breath work, or *pranayama*. Do not stress if you are not there today. For many of us shallow breathers, this is an entirely new exercise. Like anything new, practice makes us better. Continuous, focused practice makes us much better.

After the *pranayama* opening segment of this Red Grounding exercise, begin to inhale for seven and exhale for seven. Counting at first, to ensure metered breaths. Ceasing to count once breath inhalation / exhalation regularity levels have been achieved.

Now, close your eyes. See a red energy center, located at your groin area, associated with the sexual energy of human creative force, swirling and swooshing. Check in with yourself. Where are you today?

Know that extreme lustful thinking leads to lewd and lascivious compulsions. Take your sexual energy, and your co-creative authority, very seriously. Do not be frivolous with this immensely powerful, procreative force.

There is time, and a place, for human sexual expression of course. Yet, human sexual expression often gets boys and men in trouble at work, in social situations, even at family events! Seek balance as you check in with this fiery red energy center.

Begin to see and feel the red circle of energy swirling in the area of your groin. Now, om the low C note audibly. Imagining the red energetic vortex as being the size of a golf ball sphere.

Now, turn the frequency, volume, and intensity up on the low C note and enlarge that golf ball-sized sphere to the size of an orange. Turn the frequency, and intensity, volume up on the low C note. See the red energy now morph to the size of a basketball sphere.

Finally, envisage the entirety of your human bodily vessel as being engulfed within a spherical vortex of red energy that encompasses your entire body. Surge the deepest, most savage low C note that you have ever emanated forth into this wonderful world.

Vibrate the walls of your groin area. From the inside out. Feel the low C vibration in your physical human bodily vessel.

Now, bring the human bodily vessel size red energy sphere back down to the size of the basketball sphere. Now down to the size of the orange sphere. Finally, all the way back home as the size of the golf ball sphere.

Check in with your human bodily vessel energies once again.

See this continuum line in your head. At one end of the line is the number one. On the other end of the continuum line is the number ten.

One represents completely flat sexuality (no libido drive). Ten represents the highest level of sexual drive you have ever felt in your entire life.

While in your red meditation, check in with that area in your body. Where are you on the continuum? Well if you are leaning toward an eight or a nine at an inopportune time, ask your inner self for balance in that energetic area of your human bodily vessel. Balance received.

Through meditative efforts, you can learn to consciously turn down the intensity and frequency vibration of that energy center. Or any energy center for that matter. See the continuum once again in your mind's eye. Now if the current setting is at an eight. Move the setting in your mind's eye to the left six notches. Set it at a two.

That may just indeed be a much more appropriate setting for this morning's board room meeting. Set the intention for middle pillar balance. In the sexual, and all other, areas of your life.

"Hey, man. You are at a nine. I need you at a two." Set the intention for where you want to be and know why.

Let us now apply theory to practice. Where the rubber meets the road as they say.

Onward now to the play the tape all the way through decision making exercise. Use this technique whenever you make any important, and some not so important, decisions in your life going forward. Play the tape all the way through.

The Play the Tape All the Way Through, Decision Making Exercise

The Play the Tape All the Way Through, Decision Making exercise is the first of seven exercises allowing for demonstration of mastery of each of the seven powerful fatherly lessons presented within this book in real-world, real-time decision making application. You will be able to deploy and utilize this exercise within a wide variety of everyday experiences, situations, and scenarios. It is a decision making cure-all!

With no exaggeration, this one exercise alone is a panacea cure-all for the making of bad decisions. That is not to say that you will not make strategic blunders in tactical decision making along the way. To err is human.

Most of our so-called "problems" are self-created. The key to not creating the types of personal implosions is to act going forward through the art of judicious decision making. Playing the tape all the way through. This can be done far easier than you can possibly imagine.

Prior to making any decisions large or small, take pause.

Consider all of the variables. All the various permutations of reality that could come into play around the decision at hand. Literally fast forward the tape of how things will work out in your mind. Play the tape all the way through. In times of puzzlement, seek the sage advice of an older mentor who has more experience in life regarding such matters to assist with seeing the way the tape ends.

For instance, imagine you are on the horns of a dilemma. Your best friend got into a party college near your house, one you applied to as a backup in case you didn't get accepted into your first choice: a better academic university further from your hometown.

As it turned out, you ended up getting into the much more academically and socially prestigious university. The one further from home. You should of course be excited, but you are not.

One part of you wants to stay home. To throw that prestigious academic institution acceptance letter in the wastebasket. You are comfortable where you are right now. Comfortable with continuing to date your current girlfriend and with keeping your usual hangouts with your existing buddies alive and going for few more years.

Why bother pressuring yourself to excel? Or, to do something great?

You could always just slide by at the local college. You will still get a degree and a job after. Facing no stress at all whatsoever during the process for the next four years potentially! Before just pushing the easy button, go ahead and play the tape all the way through.

If you remain close by, at the party school college, and never push yourself, you will live to painfully regret that poor decision. You will have settled for the comfortable. Needily clinging, like an infant, to the familiar over the pursuance of excellence.

Play the tape all the way through. You know what happens if you stay close by at the party school. You will finish your degree, but you'll be surrounded by mediocre people, drinking heavily, and putting on weight. Like everyone else addicted to the toxic CRAP Frankenfood way of eating enfeebling the multitude.

You will have married your girlfriend, secured a job in your hometown, gotten divorced, and begun to exercise your visitation with your kids all in what will have seemed like a blink of the eye. By that time, you will be paying massive amounts of child support, and perhaps even alimony, while another man sleeps in your bed and raises your children.

Enjoy your pool view. From your studio apartment. Or, play the tape all the way through. Make a different set of decisions this time. It is up to you. Choose your own adventure, my friends.

As the second scenario plays out, you take the challenge to advance yourself by going to the more prestigious, and academically rigorous, university away from your hometown. Your girlfriend proves her metal, by sticking by your side. Or, she departs. Her decision.

Either way, you remain laser focused on the creation, and subsequent identification, of your definite life purpose in the context of your overall life mission. You strengthen your position in life always.

Play the tape all the way through again. This time you graduate from a prestigious academic university with honors. You are working full-time in a great company. Making buck. Moreover, you are in graduate school earning your master's degree in the evenings and online.

All the while, your high school best friend ended up doing time for an accident they were part of while driving under the influence near the campus of your hometown college.

This time, you married your high school sweetheart who proved herself maintaining a supportive position with absolute fidelity to you as her man ever encouraging your academic, and subsequent career, achievement. Visiting you on the weekends at your university, she went on to graduate from the college in your hometown, commanding a great salary of her own, and working in the industry of her choice.

In this second play the tape all the way through, you are both financially independent, well off by any standards of contemporary comfort. If there is a split later on down the road the breakup can be much more amicable as each person has their own resources. No one will feel the financial incentive to decapitate the other legally. Like shooting someone for their Air Jordan shoes for a windfall payout. Perverse incentives produce perverse circumstances, my friends.

Playing the tape all the way through requires self-discipline. Often times a great deal of courage as well. To really know what you want to create in this lifetime, you must follow the admonishment of Sun Tzu to know thyself so that you won't be too afraid of the battles you face.

Impulsive decisions, rooted in the convenience of pressing the easy button, are in most all situations and circumstances not the most useful long-term choice.

The key is that you must be able to forgo what it is that you want in this present moment so you can become whatever you want to be in this lifetime. In all areas of life, playing the tape all the way through is the most helpful decision-making tool there is in my arsenal. Play the tape all the way through in all areas of your life experience. Food being no exception.

Play the tape all the way through before you put carbonated/caffeinated, refined sugar, acidic, and processed foods (CRAP Frankenfoods) in your mouth.

When you play the tape all the way through you will make much better food related decisions as well.

Remember now, you are what you eat.

Lesson Two

GIGO & You Are What You Eat

During my childhood – which was really not that long ago – television programming actually provided interesting, accurate, pragmatically applicable, useful information for the citizenry.

It's funny to think about it now, but in the early 1970s, there were only a handful of television stations in existence. Television programming back then was much more standardized, predictably uniform, and, by contemporary standards, quite limited in both nature and scope.

Believe it or not, back then, television stations also actually went off the air in the wee hours of the morning.

An American flag waving proudly on a sunny day was the backdrop for station sign-off while the national anthem played. After station sign off, only a static picture and white noise audio remained. Carol Anne, are you in there? If you remember the movie "Poltergeist" you are truly showing your age!

Yet, with the reliability of the rising sun, the television stations would sign back on each morning just before daybreak.

Television sets, at that time, were nothing like the fifty-seven inch, thinly designed, smart device attached to your living room wall today. No, no, and no.

Television sets were super heavy wooden pieces of furniture with a semi-reflective, cloudy glass front when powered down. Smelling of wooden furniture polish, these clunky living room centerpieces came to life each evening. Here's an excerpt from my very favorite childhood public service infomercial.

"Take it from the Chopper, because the Chopper knows it's true. Exercise your Choppers on some good hard food" (Chopper, 1982).

Starring in that PSA was the quintessential greaser; clad in the stereotypical 1950s rolled-up cuffed jeans, t-shirt, and leather jacket of the day, that guy went by the name of Chopper which was fitting indeed because he rolled up on a chopped-out motorcycle. Chopper's jingle encouraged the audience to eat what Chopper referred to as "hard foods" – foods that require you to chew – illuminating that if you want to be cool like Chopper, then you must eat as the cool kids do. If the tough, cool, and high-octane Chopper is eating right, then so should you.

Chopper's PSA was a strong push to get the people of that time to eat more raw fruits and vegetables. Just for good measure, Chopper is shown chewing on a raw celery stick at the very end of the PSA. Where are those kinds of public service announcements today when they are needed the most?

Across my lifetime, we have seen the pedal to metal acceleration of the everyday omnipresence of CRAP Frankenfoods creeping into every nook and cranny of our society.

Processed foods have been around since the turn of the 20th century. They are nothing new. The problem today, for the vast majority of us, is that we are just eating way too much processed CRAP Frankenfood.

When I was a kid, it was very common for Westerners to replace grocery store produce with produce grown in their small plot gardens.

My grandmother had such a garden. To this day, I consider her compost-fertilized garden plot to be the most fertile land on the planet. Back then, almost everyone ate sunlight foods on a daily basis. It was what we had. Today, some boys and men go months, and even years if you can believe it, without ever consuming any sunlight whatsoever.

Overall, as a human race we have never eaten this way, folks. Perhaps someone should sound the Paul Revere alarm.

"The CRAP Frankenfoods are killing us! The CRAP Frankenfoods are killing us!"

Done.

Seriously, folks, it is as if we are wandering aimlessly, with blinders on seemingly, into unchartered territory. Quite frankly, it is high time to sound the alarm.

We have seen a striking departure from the way that humans have eaten since time immemorial over the last half-century. Human beings have gone from eating primarily sunlight foods to a straight diet of toxic CRAP Frankenfood.

Today there is an utter, and complete, disconnect in understanding of where food actually comes from among the citizenry. Nowadays, folks have little exposure to, and a complete and total lack of understanding, of the true curative nature of real whole sunlight food.

Growing up in rural Virginia, I worked at a peach orchard during the sultry summers of my wayward teenage youth. I attended 4-H camp where we learned about the farming, the environment, and the responsibility, of the whole of humankind, for mother earth stewardship.

Additionally, I was a member of my high school's Future Farmers of America (FFA). I worked harvesting white potatoes, sweet potatoes, and tomatoes during my collegiate year's summer breaks. With all of the automation of farming that has taken place, fewer young people today have the privilege of working the earth and seeing where food actually comes from.

Seeing both the sowing and the reaping of whole foods from the earth helps one to better understand the true nature of both life and the living of it.

People today simply do not understand the true nature of food. Yet, they sure do like to talk a lot about the subject.

Don't eat after six. Only eat after six.

Never eat carbohydrates before noon. Only eat carbohydrates before noon.

Count calories. Ignore calorie counting.

Focus on the BMI. Ignore the BMI.

For all the hogwash spewed, no one seems to understand anything at all whatsoever about the true nature of food these days. This is largely due to the overabundance of information that always seems to be inherently contradictory in nature, a chief characteristic of social media logic.

One thing we know for sure is that dieting doesn't work. Diets are temporary solutions to unremittingly perennial problems and challenges. Much like political parties who rant and rave going forth. Pontificating endlessly upon the great work to be done. The significant changes to be made. Who subsequently do absolutely nothing whatsoever of any real substance upon assuming power. Unbeknownst to the citizenry the political system and the CRAP Frankenfood misery industrial complex are in fact financed by the very same corporate interests.

Begin to take the helm of your own mind by first getting the toxic CRAP Frankenfood garbage out of your system. Let's face facts. None of the faddish pills sold on infomercials and in chain health food stores, are going to cut it.

It's the food, stupid. Eat whole sunlight foods. Lean heavily in the direction of primarily plant-based eating. Without hesitation, or any chicken-heartedness whatsoever, stop eating the CRAP Frankenfoods. Immediately and altogether.

The divinely masculine boy or man has beaten back the tyranny of the taste buds. CRAP Frankenfoods, masquerading as actual nutrition these days, hold absolutely no sway over him. None whatsoever. Processed foods account for most all food that comes in a box or bag these days. We eat a lot of it!

Over 75% of boys and men in the West are either overweight or obese because the vast majority of us are all eating high quantities of low-quality foods.

Wake up, gentlemen. Avoid the CRAP Frankenfood trap.

Avoiding the CRAP Frankenfood Trap

As you now know, CRAP Frankenfoods constitute the vast majority of the toxic nourishment being consumed in the West.

If you have shopped at one of the big-box stores recently, then you already well know. Obesity, and overweightness, in the West has now exceeded epidemic crisis level proportions.

The CRAP Frankenfood trap is now a stratospheric national security public health crisis. Worse yet, it is exacerbating. Much useless misinformation, and disinformation, regarding the food we eat, abounds. Similarly, there is an extreme deficit of useful information containing real facts about the highly addictive nature of sugary, chemical laden, acidic, processed CRAP Frankenfoods that are collectively poisoning us all.

CRAP Frankenfood trap avoidance measures directly center upon your ability to think outside of the box. Seeing the toxicity of the world around you. Without giving in to its insidious demands.

Acquiescing not to the omnipresence of groupthink bullying forces that would, in all complete and total honesty, smile upon your remaining in the sick zone. With the rest of them. No joke. Misery loves company, my friends. Mastery does too. Join the masters. Not the wretched. Wake up. What the heck are we all putting in our mouths?

All the myriad years of human evolution thus far have not been fueled by CRAP Frankenfoods.

On the contrary, those countless eons of human physical, intellectual, and dare I even write spiritual, evolutionary progress were exclusively fueled by sunlight foods. Emanating directly from the synergy of the sun, earth, and ether. All of the elements.

That was the very fuel that got us to the point where we have allowed Technological Enfeeblement Syndrome to cripple us. We have simply just forgotten that our very own human bodily vessels are, too, a direct emanation of the synergistic confluence of the sun, earth, and ether. In this plastic age of high technology, most human beings are extremely disconnected from the earth.

With the highest consumption rates of CRAP Frankenfood ever being consumed now in the West, there is not much hope for the population at large. As long as people keep eating the same toxic CRAP Frankenfood, no diet, workout scam, app, or self-help book will ever work for them in the leaning out game. It is the food, stupid.

Those people are what they eat. They eat CRAP Frankenfoods. Getting off the CRAP Frankenfood hamster wheel is damn-near impossible for most. They are way too programmed. Brainwashed, through taste bud tyranny, to increasingly consume more of the very same CRAP Frankenfoods that are making them so very sick in the first place. Where there is such rapacious demand, a supply chain will soon follow.

Tell that to the political theater performers we call our elected officials. The war on drugs did not work. The only public policy solution that can ever work, to address the nation's illicit drug problems, are those that serve to reduce the demand for narcotics. Yet, those types of public policies will never even be considered by our esteemed elected bodies. I wonder why not?

Term limits. Campaign finance reform.

The same goes for the omnipresence of toxic CRAP Frankenfood in our society. On one hand you hear political luminaries, and the occasional swampy bureaucrat, come out to encourage people, young people in particular, to eat healthy and exercise. The youth in America should strive earnestly to maintain a relatively healthy BMI. Yet, the food served in their school cafeterias is mostly genetically modified, corn syrup laden, toxic CRAP Frankenfood to the core.

Many American citizens, within the food deserts of violent inner cities, have little access to clean, whole nutritious foods. Chicken joints and soul food places – both chock-full of low-quality, artery clogging meat products coupled with numerous fried, gluttonous offerings of the many stripes – are all that is available in terms of nutrition for urban folk.

People in more affluent areas often have better access to high-quality, organic, non-GMO, sunlight foods, yet they are often too spoiled to go out and procure the very food that would improve all areas of their lives.

Ride the tip of the spear with many brave others, catalyzing energies of synergistic human evolutional consciousness upgrade. Start now. You can make very positive steps, in a highly fruitful way, by simply deciding right now what you are going to do and why.

To move forward along the path of Divine Masculinity, one must change his thinking about food. Most people are left unaware of just how toxic the CRAP Frankenfoods they're consuming in insanely high quantities are.

An awakening of this nature is necessary to spare another generation of human beings the suffering, pain, and eventual miserable death associated with the near exclusive consumption of CRAP Frankenfood.

This awakening has been greatly impeded, on a mass scale, by the overwhelming number of advertising dollars allocated toward the systemic, programmatic obfuscation of the true salutary nature of sunlight foods.

We have all been bamboozled. Double crossed by the very institutions that we thought had our back. Wake up. You must save your own life, if it is to be saved at all. Change your mind right now about what you consider to be food.

Only eat sunlight foods going forward, as CRAP Frankenfood will only serve to lead one down the path of suffering, sickness, and servitude. A trifecta payout to the pharmaceutical industrial complex.

After you have changed your mind about food, then, my friends, embark to change your mind about the snake oil pharmaceutical solutions that are proffered as antidotes for the sicknesses and malaise brought about by the continuous consumption of CRAP Frankenfood. It's the food, stupid!

It is all so bizarre. Yet, when you take a few steps back and look at all of this lunacy from afar, it all comes into focus. We are being fed toxic CRAP Frankenfood on the front end where big corporations, who do not have our best health interests in mind, are making quite the profit by literally fattening up the American people for the harvest.

Then, to add insult to injury, the citizenry is given band-aid solutions: ridiculously profitable pharmaceutical antidotes for the CRAP Frankenfood poisoning most often coming with horrible side effects. The types of side effects that require more prescription pills.

Get off this hamster wheel, gentlemen. It is killing you. Literally.

The vast majority of the medications being prescribed simply allow people to continue to fuel their addiction to the toxic CRAP Frankenfoods. The very same toxic CRAP Frankenfoods that are making all of them so very sick in the first place!

Wake up. Save your own life. Change your thinking about pharmaceutical industrial complex solutions to self-imposed, toxic CRAP Frankenfood consumption.

Danger, Will Robinson! (Beware Snake Oil Pharmaceutical Solutions)

Many of you readers have picked up on the fact that I use the phrase "Danger, Will Robinson." I suspect most of my younger readers in particular have no idea from where that phrase originated. So, I will let the cat out of the bag about Will Robinson.

"Danger, Will Robinson" was a phrase uttered by a robot guardian and travel companion, a space-age chaperone, for the main character (Will Robinson) of the 1960s hit show *Lost in Space.* That show ran, as a re-run, during the early to mid-1970s.

In today's urban dictionary parlance, that phrase has a twenty-first century translation. It means, "Hey, lookout! You are about to do something really stupid." The phrase "Danger, Will Robinson" is completely apropos here. We have all been collectively buffaloed to take the snake oil pharmaceutical correctives for our pandemic CRAP Frankenfood enslavement.

What the heck are we doing? We know gosh darn well that the CRAP Frankenfood we have allowed ourselves to become so horribly addicted to is making us all sick. Yet, we continue merrily down the path of kissing the ring of our tyrannical taste buds.

There are a multitude of pharmaceutical industrial complex snake oil pill remedies that will allow you to subsist in a tubby human bodily vessel for many years to come. Joints aching, as you waddle from your couch to the refrigerator, while shopping online on your iPhone.

Note to self. Don't forget to verify your synchronous video e-appointment with the urologist next week. You need the erectile disfunction medicine to further fuel your pornography addiction. Don't you know?

Got psoriasis? No problem. Don't change anything you are eating at all. Nothing whatsoever. No need. We have a pill for that.

A1C levels too high. No worries there. Keep eating the same CRAP Frankenfood. We have a pill for that one too.

Erectile dysfunction kicking in? Who doesn't need a boost from an erectile dysfunction pill to really get the blood flowing after dining out on toxic CRAP Frankenfood on a Saturday night? Of course, we have pills for that one too!

Before you know it, you will be adding blood pressure medications, cholesterol-lowering drugs, statins, which require an additional CoQ10 pill, and so forth and so on. You see where this is all going, don't you?

Eventually, and before you know it, you will be taking a pill to counteract the side effects of another pill. Trust me, I get it. I was once very much on the sickness path as well.

I changed my life through redefining and reconceptualizing the notion of food. My new hard and fast rule: I eat sunlight foods.

Eat Sunlight Foods

Sunlight foods are the exact diametrical one hundred eighty degree polar shift opposite to CRAP Frankenfoods. The technological advances achieved over the past century have conferred great advantages for all of us. Concomitantly, in parallel fashion as a collective, humanity has become more disconnected from the earth, and ourselves, than ever. The synergy of earth and sun produce the highest quality of curative, life-enhancing foods known to man.

Yet, today's everyday mundane, humdrum human being has little or no understanding whatsoever about the salutary nature of real food. What real food actually is and from where it originates seems to be a cryptogrammatic riddle for people today.

This is due largely to the fact that all the generations, subsequent to my Generation X, have only known toxic processed foods for the entirety of their gormandizing lives.

CRAP Frankenfoods grown from genetically modified organism (GMO) seeds. Laden with high fructose corn syrup. You know, that nasty sap that makes everything taste good? Code for addiction by the way. We are being poisoned, my friends.

The extremely high rate of overweight and obese people in the United States correlates with the high levels of refined sugars contained within the poisonous, chemical-laden, processed CRAP Frankenfood Western diet that we are all taking in so very blindly. We have all allowed ourselves to fall into the trap of eating refined sugar laden processed CRAP Frankenfoods in lieu of actual real, organic, non-GMO sunlight foods. We are surely paying a high price for such a decision.

Sunlight foods are organic, non-GMO foods that come direct from the earth's sunlight synergy. Organic salsa with non-GMO corn chips is an example of sunlight foods. Rice noodle vegetarian lasagna, topped with vegan plant cheese, served alongside gluten-free bread is an example of a tasty sunlight food prepared dish.

A great sunlight food lunch is toasting a cauliflower rice hamburger bun and grilling up a meatless, organic bean burger to put inside. Top it with raw organic tomatoes and lettuce, alongside non-GMO French fries that you made yourself at home, and voilà. A perfect sunlight foods lunch is born.

When it comes to the consumption of food, I live by three rules.

1. I am primarily plant-based, and I eat non-GMO verified sunlight foods. Primarily plant-based means what it says. I chose my words carefully today, my friends. I don't mean vegan. I don't mean vegetarian. Gathering to throw paint on unsuspecting perambulators in a public square because they are wearing fur is no way to proselytize. No way at all. Primarily plant-based eating is apolitical. It is just hands down the healthiest way for humans, of any of the political stripes, to chow down.

2. I eat only rice cauliflower breads. Most breads fall into the category of processed foods. When I think breads, I think puffy. Imagine the Pillsbury Dough Boy. He wasn't exactly thin, tan, and toned. Was he? Yeast expands. Processed yeast paste is simply no longer welcome in my sacred human bodily vessel. Consider barring it from your own.

3. I eat all the junk food I want. As long as I cook it myself that is for sure! I buy organic sweet potatoes. I love cutting them all up. Fry them in coconut oil. Have away. They are delicious! For a tasty dessert, place an acai berry base in a bowl. Top it with gluten-free, organic granola and bananas. Have at it. All day long.

Take control of your weight, body image, and start the leaning out. Begin today. Eat healthier fats and proteins in lieu of refined sugary products. I like to snack on non-GMO nuts, of all varieties, all day long! My intuition tells me they are brain food. What does your gut tell you?

You can do this.

If you are to live happy, healthy, and free in a human bodily vessel capable of the highest levels of sacred vibratory energetic conductivity you must undertake the self-refinement work. For inspiration, look no further than one of my favorite childhood cartoons, Popeye the Sailor Man.

The Popeye Ate Spinach Story

"I am Popeye the Sailor Man. I am strong to the finish because I eat my spinach. I am Popeye the Sailor Man" (Popeye, 1943). Popeye the Sailor Man was a popular cartoon character emanating back from the 1920s. Popeye cartoon re-runs from the 1950s and 1960s were still very popular daytime cartoon programming in the early 1970s. Popeye was awesome.

He was a salt-of-the-earth, hardworking, decent sort of chap. His signature move was to pop open a can of spinach when he needed strength and stamina to take on challenges of life. Such as his inevitable confrontations with his archnemesis, Brutus.

Popeye ate his greens. Popeye prospered. That was the simple moral of the story. You hear a lot of talk these days, in dietary and nutritionist circles, about the advantages of *this* type of diet over *that* type of diet. It is never just as simple to eat healthy, organic, non-GMO sunlight foods now, is it?

Of course not. Silly me. It has to be much more obfuscating. If we told the truth, it would take down the multi-billion dollar fad diet industrial complex altogether. People would be out of work! Throw out Occam's razor altogether.

Let us divert our time, attention, and money to the studies produced by the experts who will tell us what to do and why. They know what is best for us. Beware the nonpartisan, objective group of experts. They are usually funded by, and in league with, a highly partisan group of experts. Profiteering PhD-educated statisticians are all too venally willing to bend the raw data. In whatever direction the money trail directs them. This is all a sham sideshow distraction to keep you occupied with nonsense, spinning circles in your head to ensure that you don't take the time to see through the logical fallacies. Fallacious arguments so strikingly apparent when your eyes are open to the truth.

All of the expert talk, the ridiculous argumentation, and the overwhelming amount of information inundating studies and analyses are meant to do one thing. One thing only. To muddy the water. To obfuscate. It's a smokescreen by design.

The arguments that these so-called dietary and nutritional experts pontificate over and argue about ad infinitum, often quite vociferously, are all misleading. It is a programmed narrative meant to keep tackling the same set of problems over and over without ever solving them. The solving of such problems would of course put them all out of business. They are in the tackling business.

This is the illusion. See through it now.

Wake up. Stop eating CRAP Frankenfoods immediately. Eat whole sunlight foods. Eat live foods. Eat natural anti-inflammatory and antioxidant foods. Sunlight foods enliven the human bodily vessel. Acidic inflammatory processed CRAP Frankenfoods serve only to enfeeble the human bodily vessel long term.

Face it here, folks. Popeye had it right!

The key here is to eat as many fresh organic vegetables, fruits, beans, and lentils as possible. Avoiding the CRAP Frankenfood trap altogether. Even citrus fruits, which are highly acidic outside of the human bodily vessel, promote alkalinity upon ingestion.

So, instead of making a run for the border for a late-night Mexican-style CRAP Frankenfood, think ahead. You should already have the ingredients you will need for an organic bean burrito at your house. Prepare healthy foods for yourself at your home. Most all Westerners spend a ton of money eating out. Expensive coffee-based, sugary crap drinks in the morning. Processed fast food for lunch. Gluttonous dinners out.

Don't forget all the deliveries. Spending has increased in this area of consumption due to the rise of delivery services. These so-called services will actually pick up all types of CRAP Frankenfoods, bringing them directly to your door. As you lay paunchy, and potbellied, on your mother's couch.

Think about it. The average Westerner spends up to ten bucks, or more, on their super mocha frappa crappa latte highly caffeinated and highly acidic brew of morning death punch. Many Westerners easily spend twenty to twenty-five dollars or more (I am seriously being conservative here with my estimates) on their processed meat lunches and other snacks on the daily. If the person is a cigarette smoker, or a vaper, add another five to that total number.

Given what I have just written, it is hilarious to me that the most frequent response that I get when I tell people to start eating organic, non-GMO foods, which are of course primarily fresh fruits and vegetables, is that it is too expensive. "Oh no, I could never afford that!"

My response is that they cannot not afford it. Yes, I'll admit, eating organic, non-GMO foods will cost you a ton more at the grocery store. I get it. Good food is expensive. You should spend the lion's share of your monthly food budget on whole, organic, non-GMO foods.

If you cut out the CRAP Frankenfood you purchase, pack a nutritious lunch for yourself daily, and cook your evening meals and nightly snacks at home, you will actually save a ton of money in the end.

Moreover, you will not end up paying the same insane amounts for doctor visits or prescription drugs as you did prior to walking the primarily plant-based way of being.

Remember the two old adages: garbage in, garbage out (GIGO) and you are what you eat.

When you stop to consider how much money you are actually spending on CRAP food currently and how much money you will spend in effort to alleviate the pain, suffering, and malaise that will inevitably be bestowed upon you if you continue eating CRAP Frankenfood, you will clearly see that proactively adopting a primarily plant-based way of being is the most useful, and appropriate, means of fueling your human bodily vessel toward health, wealth, and happiness in this lifetime going forth.

Face it, folks. You are what you eat. You don't want to be solely constituted by refined sugars, do you?

You Are What You Eat Exercise 2: Refined Sugars

In Lesson Two, I have broken down the deleterious nature of what I refer to as CRAP Frankenfoods. Let's get to the R in CRAP!

The second You Are What You Eat exercise focuses upon refined sugars. Refined sugars are found in almost all processed foods. Processed, as I have made mention previously in this work, are those foods that come in boxes, bags, and cans. Literally, food that has been processed. Most all fast food is considered to be processed.

We have all been hoodwinked. We have all been collectively blank-slated. We have forgotten where food comes from.

The second of the You Are What You Eat exercises challenges you to stop eating refined sugars altogether. Your challenge is to consume healthier fats and proteins such as nuts, avocado, and legumes. Flip the script on your unruly, spoiled taste buds and let them know they no longer hold power over you. Your taste buds are meant to be servants, vetting tools for food quality.

Be sure of one thing: cessation of refined sugars will suck. At least at first. Your brain, like that of a crack addict or chain-smoking cigarette fiend, will have you nearly convinced that eating junk food once again is a good idea.

Resist.

Be rebellious. Do not acquiesce no matter how loud that voice in your head gets.

I suggest that when you begin to walk this path, you completely throw out all of the CRAP Frankenfood from your refrigerator, freezer, and cupboard shelves.

Respect thyself. Respect others. If you live with other suffering human beings, especially if it is not your own house, be considerate knowing that the other members of that household may not be on your karmic path.

Those folks may not be hearing the clarion call to change their lives for the better by eating real, live, raw foods. They simply are not ready to raise their bodily vessel vibrations to allow energy to flow from heel to crown and back down.

Walk your path. Eat your sunlight foods. Do not expect others to do what you are doing. Do not expect others to eat what you are eating. Do not try to convince anyone of the superiority of your new ways of thinking. Demonstrate. Do not explicate. When the results are in, they will soon enough be coming to you. Allow that to transpire.

Proselytizing doesn't really work anyway. Unsolicited proselytizing has an even worse success rate!

Get back to the basics, gentlemen. Adopt a walking practice in your life. Your daily and nightly perambulations are healing on multiple levels. Seen and unseen.

Workout Exercise 2: Walking

Workout Exercise Two focuses on walking. I know what some of you are thinking already. Walking? Who the heck wants to walk? I get it. Trust me, I understand.

Having wheels represents freedom. Freedom to leave the confines of your parental domestic circle. To go outside the wire. Getting out and hitting the open road. To feel like you are your own man.

I will never forget the day I turned fifteen years and eight months. I was up with the roosters, dressed, and finger tapping a dent into the kitchen table, as I waited for my mother to get ready to drive me to the DMV. That was the fateful day I was to take the written and driving portions of the learner's permit test.

Long story short, all went well that morning. I had seriously studied for the learner's permit driving test. Memorizing all relevant distances, lights, signs, maneuvers, and standard operating procedures.

I knew that tattered study book inside and out. Having perused its contents for months in preparation for that fateful day. The day I was to sit and prove both my written competency and actual driving skills to the world. Envisaging myself in the lineage of Richard Petty, I embarked on this once and a lifetime rite of passage. From passenger to driver.

Remember if you fail to plan, you plan to fail. Set a definite purpose and achieve it.

Even though I couldn't wait back then to get my learner's permit and then my own driver's license, I walk today more often than I drive whenever possible. I do in fact own a truck, but I choose to walk for my health, wealth, and happiness. Give it a try.

Consider the reasons you should commit to an everyday walking practice to enhance your physical, emotional, and spiritual life resilience.

Physically, walking is a relatively low-impact exercise. It is great cardio. Moreover, when done right, it can be a walking meditation.

Keep an open mind here. Think of our human ancestors. They walked miles upon miles each day. Hunting and gathering. Subsistence farming.

For millennia, my friends. Eons and eons.

Homo sapiens were not structurally engineered to remain in stationary positions. Not for hours on end, staring at the screens of all our fancy devices. Absorbed in our smart device is no way to go through life.

We were engineered to be agile, mobile, resilient, and versatile. How much of that do you see anymore?

Not so unexpectedly, much of the disease, despair, and malaise today is totally correlated with the sedentary lifestyle. Think outside the box. Know to walk your human bodily vessel each day. Stretch out the muscles. Unplug from your smart devices.

It is also nice to walk with others who have removed their own electronic leashes for the duration of the stroll.

During your daily, or nightly, perambulations, talk to your fellow walkers. Really listen to their words. Feel the emotional, communicative connection. Get to know, and understand, your fellow ambulatory interlocutors.

Unplug. Do not even take your cell phone along with you. Unless, of course, you do so for safety reasons.

Give unplugging a chance. The relief is immediate and refreshing. Really give this a go. Begin walking three miles each day. In conjunction with your meditative practice and Five Tibetan practice, your walking and sunlight food eating will have you shedding pant sizes.

Soon enough you'll be trimmer than you have been in a long time. You will be comfortable taking off your shirt going for a run, to yoga, or to the beach. The work is worth it. Do the work.

Emotionally, most people are carrying a ton of baggage resulting from years of horribly negative, toxic programming. Walking alone has great curative benefits in itself. It helps catalyze release.

On your nightly, device free perambulations, you'll have time to review the day behind you. Free of noises, voices, energetic stressors, and myriad other external phenomena.

You have time to consider how well you really tried that morning during your Five Tibetan and meditative exercises. Were they full-on or were they half-baked? Who benefits from it being full-on? You know.

Then, you should consider how you reacted to the various stimuli and personalities that came across your path during your day. Where did your attachments shine right on through? Were you fearful? Defensive? Insecure? Perhaps even snarky? How could you move forward not making that mistake, or similar mistakes, again?

As you continue your perambulation, you can get into you own personal strategic life planning efforts. Do you have a definite life purpose in the overall context of your life mission? If not, get one. Walking unplugged gives you the time for inner-work reflection allowing you to see where you are going and why.

People these days are often quite confused about the very nature of emotions. Emotional reactivity in human beings is running rampant. Upset people upset people.

Sick human beings relish in being downtrodden and morose. It is their way. Avoid them, or at least, limit your exposure. Other human beings are just so stressed they freak out to the point where they are emotionally on edge. All the time!

Unplugging on an evening walk allows for you to regain self-perspective, seeing where you are currently in juxtaposition to where you really want to be. Knowing both where you are now and where you are going. How rare is that these days!

With a solid action plan consisting of logical, progressive steps forward, marching ever steadily toward one's definite life purpose in the overall context of one's life mission is emotionally quite comforting as opposed to living your life strapped to an emotional roller coaster.

Walk unplugged. Do the introspective planning work that will take you to the next level. Focus on your breathing. Inhaling and exhaling deeply as you lengthen your stride and walk home with a strong gait. You will find that walking is indeed a spiritual practice as well.

You hear phrases such as walking the spiritual path. Mindful walking is a moving meditation. Walking alone, or in intentional noble silence with a meditative walking group, is uplifting to the soul. Give this a try.

Leave the confines of your dwelling. Walk off the electronic leashing and experience the natural rhythms of the outside world around you. Walking is a form of grounding yourself to the earth beneath you. You come from the earth. You will eventually return to the earth.

Make the time above ground count. Practice meditating on a daily basis to allow for a blanket of serenity. It will greatly assist in the weathering of the storm in this rancorous age. You do not have to react to external stimuli. You can be free, liberated from the reactivity of the monkey mind. Go inward. Go deep. Learn to meditate.

Meditation Exercise Two: Orange

Begin Meditation Exercise Two with the same warm-up pranayama breathing exercise that you learned at the outset of Meditation Exercise One. Inhale deeply and then exhale. Expand your lung capacity each meditative session. Allow for massive amounts of oxygen to fuel and heal your human bodily vessel. At the completion of your deepest inhalation, aiming for twenty-one counts like before, return to normal metered breaths. Settle into your meditative position, either seated on the floor or in a chair, with your spine straight, chin up, and eyes closed.

Envisage an orange-hued energy center located just below your belly button. Begin to move your vibrational intonations up to the low D note. Om the low D note aloud. Feel it vibrating your orange energetic center. You will know that you have hit the right low D intonation when you feel the low D vibration just beneath the navel, invigorating and enlivening that orange energy center.

Awaken. Where are you today?

Remember that the orange energy center is associated with the deadly sin of gluttony and the virtue of temperance. As always, you want to be in the leanest, lightest, and strongest human bodily vessel possible to maximize your life experience. If your end game is health, wealth, and happiness, wake up.

Realize that without strong individual robust health and physical fitness, wealth is useless. When you are first starting out on the path to primarily plant-based eating, you will be severely tested. The delirium tremens of CRAP Frankenfood deprivation await. The meditation exercise that follows will provide relief during such weaning off of CRAP Frankenfood.

Becoming aware of the energetic centers, located within your own human bodily vessel, will greatly assist in the effort to surmount the challenges of recovery from CRAP Frankenfood addiction.

Envisage now a golf ball size orange sphere at the point of your navel. Enlarge that orange energetic sphere to the size of an orange sphere. Now, further augment the orange energic sphere up to the size of the spherical basketball.

You remember what is next. Envisage the orange energy sphere surrounding your human bodily vessel. Hear a resounding thunderous cry of the low D note in your internal amplifier. Match that intonation. Om the low D note aloud. Feel the orange vibrations at the navel, knowing you, not your spoiled taste buds, are running the eating show henceforth. You are done with self-sabotage, with ambushing thyself daily with CRAP Frankenfoods.

Now, reduce the orange energy sphere down in size to about that of a basketball. Down to the size of an orange. Finally, reduce it to about the size of a golf ball.

Where are you today when it comes to gluttony? Say you are at a number seven. See the continuum line in your head and use your mind's eye to adjust the thermostat of gluttony down from a seven to a notch of one.

Seek balance. Ask for balance.

It is done.

Now, on to the Sunlight Food (Not Frankenfood) Exercise.

The Sunlight Food (Not Frankenfood) Exercise

This is the second of seven exercises that will allow you to apply what you have learned in each of the seven lessons in this book to real-world decision-making applications. This exercise is titled the Sunlight Food (Not Frankenfood) exercise. Let's get to it.

The final exercise challenge of Lesson Two is to make a list of all the foods that you really like. Write them down, my friends. As many as you can.

Then, go to the closest health-conscious grocery store to procure the necessary organic grocery supplies to make three meals a day and a couple days worth of snacks as well. All for the upcoming week.

I like to do this on Sundays. That way, I have the entire afternoon to get all of my errands done, get my To-Do list taken care of, and prepare myself for the week.

Develop your own success patterns accordingly, depending on the start of your work week or start of your school week. If you are in school full-time, consider that to be your full-time job. Take your studies seriously. Knowledge is power, my friends.

When you arrive at the grocery store, head straight to the water section. Load your cart with seven gallons of the water of your choice (I prefer alkaline). Do your own water research. Whatever water you choose – for your own very strong, well-researched, and thought out reasons – will be important. Commit right now to drinking a gallon of water daily at the bare minimum. Once your cart is full of the gallons, head towards the produce section.

Once there, pick up three or more containers of organic baby spinach to serve as the foundational base for the salads you will be eating for dinner each evening during the upcoming week. Get all the non-GMO, organic peppers, cucumbers, potatoes, tomatoes, lettuce, radishes, mushrooms, avocado, and whatever else your heart desires to put atop your bed of baby spinach. Stack them high!

I also recommend getting the vegan plant-based dressings, found in the refrigerated section of grocery stores, to flavor those nightly salads. They are delish!

Great. Step one complete.

You now have the fixings needed to prepare a nightly dinner salad for yourself.

Once you are done getting produce, go look for the breads. Find gluten free, non-GMO, hamburger and hotdog buns. Get one of each. Put them in your cart. Find the plant-based hotdogs and the plant-based hamburgers of your choice. Put them in the cart. Then pick up some organic ketchup and mustard to use as condiments. Add in some organic non-GMO nuts, and some organic non-GMO potato chips in the basket.

Voila! You have the materials needed to pack your lunches for the next week. Now, head to the refrigerated section of the store and put some almond, coconut, oat, or soy milk in your cart.

Once that is done, pick up some organic granola for your morning meals. Organic bananas go great cut on top of granola, so pick some of those up as well. Bam. Breakfast for the next week is in the bag.

Consider getting some herbal teas (non-caffeinated, of course) for before bed relaxation and as a reward for sticking to the elevated eating path. For making it! For forging through your day, unreactive to the wild world swirling all around you.

Sweeten the tea with just a smidge of local honey. As your taste buds reconstitute themselves, through healing and cellular relearning, you will really begin to taste the honey in your tea. As if for the very first time.

Enjoy the alchemical processes of spiritual transmutation. Manifest your definite life purpose in the context of your overall life mission. Learn to sow.

Lesson Three

Learn To Sow

The divinely masculine boy or man has learned to sow. He is in charge of his life. Well on the path to the achievement of his major definite life purpose in the context of his overall life mission. He knows what he is doing. He knows why.

Know thyself. It starts with your own physical, mental, and emotional health and wellbeing. Along that vein, what has happened to the drive boys and men had to keep up high levels of physical fitness these days? Moreover, where is the entrepreneurial drive among boys and men today?

The Presidential Physical Fitness Award program was still up and running strong when I was growing up in the eighties. If you did a certain number of pull-ups, sit-ups, and beat the clock in the running race, you could earn a Presidential Physical Fitness Award patch to sew onto your winter jacket. I would like to see President Trump reinstate the Presidential Physical Fitness Award program. The nation sure needs it today!

Back then, there were different levels of Presidential Physical Fitness Award patches that were awarded based on performance, not feelings or identifications, but on actual competitive performance. Boys competed against other boys and girls competed against other girls.

The level one Presidential Physical Fitness Award patch was awarded to only the very best finishers, which were the top five percent or so. It was a high honor.

The level two patches, which were still pretty darn good, were earned by competitors who did well, just not as well as the level one patch earners.

The level three patch recipients, or bronze medalists for Olympic comparison, came in with combined event scores just beneath level two patch winners. Bear in mind that even the level three patch winners of my childhood would absolutely run circles around any kids of comparable age and gender today. People were much more fit in those times.

Moreover, at that time – prepare to gasp – the vast majority of the kids did not win a patch at all. Everyone did not get a trophy in those days. It was a better time when people were actually told the truth about their real world performance because it presented them with opportunities to improve and receive feedback based on honest performance. That type of constructive criticism is a rare gift in this day and age where we walk on eggshells to avoid being called a racist, sexist, misogynist, xenophobe, whatever the heck everyone's calling each other, seemingly all the time, now. Wake up people. Get a grip!

All three levels of Presidential Physical Fitness Award patches were set at a very high bar on purpose to push kids forward and to train year-round to win a higher-level patch in the forthcoming school year. What has happened to the indefatigable will that used to characterize the very heartbeat of America?

Has the divinely masculine drive for justice, liberty, and badass creation just been jettisoned by the wayside? Permanently? No, I think not.

There are many boys and men, across the fruited plain, on the precipice to awaken their inner divine masculine higher selves. The path of divine masculinity is the true path to lasting happiness, punctuated with sublime moments of bliss.

The divinely masculine boy or man pushes forward, inexorably testing himself and remaining steady under pressure. Possibly because he has trained under the most arduous conditions possible, failure is simply not an option. The divinely masculine man or boy has learned to sow.

And he reaps what he has sown. He holds himself, his words, and his actions accountable to the highest levels of integrity.

Just to clear up any definitional ambiguities from the outset, sowing refers to planting, and reaping refers to harvesting what has been planted. It is an agrarian metaphor, gentlemen. Terms I am sure you have heard along your path.

You reap what you sow. That would make sense, would it not? Consider now the garden scenario.

If you fail to plant the seeds correctly, fail to water the garden, and fail to pull the weeds, how can you possibly expect to glean a great, abundant harvest? You cannot.

Let us flip the switch here now. Drawing a clear parallel between the manner in which we self-govern ourselves and the seeds that we sow in life itself from this new perspective, let us play the tape all the way through. Let us see the synergistic consequences of our thoughts, words, and actions. It will all become apparent when the seeds we have sown rise from the earth and ripen.

For instance, if you sit around playing video games all day, eating CRAP Frankenfoods, and being narcissistically sloppy with your digital footprint impressions, what do you expect you will get out of this lifetime? What types of seeds are you sowing?

Can you really expect a great and abundant harvest of friends, companions, and loved ones in a time of trouble, turmoil, or sheer terror?

If you are being honest with yourself, you cannot have this expectation. You simply have not done the work. It is all actually quite elementary, my dear Watson. We reap what we sow. It is easy to understand this notion conceptually speaking, yet, knowing it at the core of your viscera is a whole different story.

Nevertheless, when people truly wake up to the realization that we are the sum of our thoughts, words, and actions, it can be absolutely life changing, in momentous fashion!

This information is free and readily available to everyone. Yet, few will learn it, even fewer will live it.

We live in a world today wherein vast numbers of boys and men do the very minimum with their lives. Flitting away their precious time by playing video games, bar-hopping around town, or just letting themselves get sucked into the misery of others.

The vast majority of boys and men are not on the path of creation for new, bold entrepreneurial ideas. The types of visionary ideas that will shape the economy just on the near horizon. Nope. Most new-fashioned modernized boys and men are just going along with the groupthink crowd, the autonomous herd. Only a tiny fraction of boys and men will actually wake up in this lifetime. Be one of them!

Become the force that your highest self-interest longs to fulfill. With pressing urgency. With indefatigable willingness. Few boys and men really live to the fullest as of late, pushing themselves to new limits.

Be one of those people, and awaken. Then, set the example for others.

Learn to sow, and then reap, when it comes to your health, career, and every other part of your life.

Truly understanding the real differences between sowing and reaping requires an understanding of the importance of earning rather than making money.

In recognition of the eminent spiritual teacher from the mid-twentieth century, Earl Nightingale, I have included his teaching from the awesome audio entitled "The Strangest Secret." I highly encourage each and every one of you to listen to this audio online.

Make a habit of regularly listening to "The Strangest Secret." It will absolutely change your life. Trust me. There are some serious golden nuggets in that recording. One such nugget has to do with the earning, not the making, of money.

Nightingale brings it to our attention that we all need to stop talking about the notion of "making money." Nightingale argues that only people who work in the mint actually make money.

For the rest of us, we must earn money!

It is important you learn a very valuable lesson about money. Do not delude yourself. Prison yards, unemployment offices, skid rows, and homeless camps are all chock full of boys and men with the innate talent, energy, and motivation to create the lives of their dreams. Those boys and men just had it wrong about this one thing. They were trying to make money. Instead, they should have learned to earn it.

Internalize this lesson: *money must be earned.*

You earn money through the provision of a useful service, product, or idea that other people find to be worthy of monetary exchange. Through your ingenuity and cultivation of greatness within yourself, you figure out what your best skill sets are and you capitalize on them.

What are your best skill sets? What types of innate talents do you possess? How are you cultivating those congenital talents? How are you benefiting from your craft? How are you advancing your definite life purpose forward? How are you taking it to the next level?

If you are an average lawyer, you may break fifty thousand dollars, give or take, in annual salary. That salary changes if you are a highly specialized lawyer – say an attorney – who is also a PhD chemist serving as the leading subject matter expert (SME) on lead poisoning class action lawsuits against well-insured municipalities. Well then, your specific knowledge and expertise may pay out an annual sum of ten times that of the average general practice attorney.

It is truly up to you to save your own life. If your dreams are to come about at all, it shall be through your personal strategic life planning, the development of your ability to control your emotions, and your due diligence as you pursue your definite life purpose.

Remember always and forever, from this day forward, that you earn money; you do not make money. The solitary internalization of that very basic axiomatic life principle alone is a game changer for many boys and men. Consider also how your ideas of making money, rather than earning money, have shackled you to mediocrity in the past? How has that limited your true self-actualization?

If you have the capacity to be completely honest with yourself, you will have to admit that your old ways of being have truly served to stultify the advancement of your life health, wealth, and happiness. You are on the road to eradicating and eviscerating the mediocre mentality from your system, purging it bit by bit. Once eradicated, never again allow that mentality to take root in your body, mind, and soul garden. Vow it, never again.

Sow then reap, my friends.

Sow then Reap

First and foremost, I encourage you to develop a personal strategic life plan, or PSLP (Check out my book, entitled *The Success Book: Developing Your Own Personal Strategic Life Plan*, available online and in fine booksellers coast to coast). Having a PSLP will provide you with a roadmap for the manifestation of the types of health, wealth, and happiness that you ordered up on life's menu of delights.

If you don't know where you are going, then you don't know where you are going. Admit it. Own it. It is far better to just make the bold admission to yourself out loud right now that you do not know what you are doing, or even where you are going, in life. Whew! You said it. What a relief. At least now you can stop pretending!

Rather than continuing to stumble forward in life, completely deluding yourself, and fooling only the inept around you, use *The Success Book: Developing Your Own Personal Strategic Life Plan* as a guide along the path to personal strategic life planning. It is a short read and you will be glad you did!

Begin today.

Do not go out partying it up tonight. Power down your phone and other smart devices. Place them in a closet, drawer, or somewhere else out of sight. Take the time to really determine what your major life purpose is and why. See how your major life purpose fits into the context of your overall life mission. True lasting happiness and awakened bliss awaits only those boys and men who choose to cultivate themselves and advance spiritually through introspective self-refinement. Sit down. Develop your own PSLP today.

Think of a ship leaving a harbor. This particular ship has no definite purpose and no destination in mind, no captain at the helm. No computerized control system. No remote-control technology to guide that vessel in any way, shape, or form. You just point the ship out of the harbor, turn on the engines, and let it go. This is another of the Nightingale teachings, by the way.

What will happen to such a ship? Will it make it safely to another harbor? Probably not. That is because the ship has no destination in mind. Without navigational guidance, that ship will, in all probable likelihood, run aground. Ending up a derelict, awaiting rescue.

The same holds true with your life. Think of yourself, of your human bodily vessel, as being the vessel of the ship. If you set forth in life with no real destination in mind, flirting with bad ideas all along the way, and going with the crowd groupthink, you may just as well end up a derelict as well. Run aground, going nowhere. You too will be awaiting rescue from others. It is often a long wait!

Figure out where you are going and why. Do not get lost in the social media programming. It is all a smoke and mirrors, my friends. Smoke screen distractions. Wake up. Pay attention. Get to work on yourself. Begin today. Be a better manager of your own time.

Your time is your most valuable resource.

Manage it well, and you will manifest stratospheric success in this lifetime.

Manage it poorly, and you will be mediocre in most all areas of your life.

Most boys and men tend to waste considerable amounts of time and energy on the melodramatic affairs of others. That is just too high a price to pay, my friends.

Where in your life have you allowed energy vampires to siphon off your precious life force in the past? Rid yourself of those social, and other, entanglements.

Simply put, some of the nouns in your life - the people, places, and things - are limiting your intellectual, physical, and spiritual development, capping your capacity well below greatness. See the realities and make changes accordingly.

Allocating your precious life force energy to address the affairs of others is simply too high a price to pay. Claim social bankruptcy, if need be. You can always rebuild your life with a new foundation predicated upon a much healthier set of assumptions regarding life, and the living of it, going forward. It is on you. Get to work. Get to the gold as the crow flies.

As the crow flies is an archaic expression for covering the distance between two points in the shortest possible amount of time. In life, get to your gold – your life purpose – straight away. Do not dilly dally. Do not wander off. Avoid distraction land as if your very life depends on it. It just may.

One big caveat. Be warned. One of the biggest impediments to the achievement of your vision of your definite purpose life mission is Technological Enfeeblement Syndrome. People often become consumed by TES, like zombies. They literally do not know that they do not know. Where in life do you not know that you don't know? Beware the pitfalls of TES. They are insidious, my friends.

Technological Enfeeblement Syndrome (TES) Avoidance Measures

The very best way to avoid contracting TES is to get back to basics. Imagine the life that I lived as a youngster coming up in the 1970s and early 1980s. There were far fewer distractions at that time. The technologies of today were nonexistent.

Most kids in America at that time read books. On rainy days, when we couldn't go outside to play, my brother and I would read volumes of the encyclopedias that stretched the entire length of the bookshelf in the den of our house. There was usually one television per house back then. Ruled by the parental units. There were no cell phones, but we had house phones called landlines.

As a young buck, if I wanted to place a call on my landline to Julie Tinker to inquire about meeting up at the Dream Roller Rink Friday evening, there was a real good chance her father would answer the landline phone.

Landline phones were often attached to the kitchen wall and a long spring cord ran from the wall mount to the base of the phone. This allowed your mother or father to cook, pinning the long-corded phone receiver between their neck and left shoulder. Stirring away. Chatting through the steamy aroma of a warm home-cooked dinner. Yes, people used to cook too!

The other phone was typically placed in a common area of the home such as the den or living room. Either way, as you see, there was little, or no, privacy.

When I set out to phone up Julie Tinker, I knew darn well that actually connecting with her was a fifty-fifty proposition on any given day. Depending, and contingent, largely upon Mr. Tinker's mood.

Mr. Tinker's gruff voice. "Hello?"

I would ask, "Is Julie there."

He would ask in reply, "Do you have a job?"

"No, sir."

"Well then, call back when you get one."

Click.

Dial tone.

I'd hang up the phone, wait, and try again a few days later.

The point here is that people of my generation, the Generation Xers, are the absolute last of the Mohicans from a technological standpoint. We were the absolute last generation on Earth to have been inculcated, programmed, and acculturated prior to the omnipresent dominance of TES. We came just prior to the digital age.

We had no movies on demand like we do now. They used to come to the local theater which opened only on Friday, Saturday, and Sunday nights. If you missed the movie in the theater, or just did not have the cash to go, then you would have to wait for the movie to be released on Home Box Office (HBO). Yes, the very same HBO that you know of today. It used to be a much bigger deal though back in that time. It had a bit of a monopoly on home movies going there for a while.

Full admission, in my late teenage years, I was able to rent movies, on VHS (video home system) tapes from the local Radio Shack or Blockbuster Video. Radio Shack is apparently still around, having made the transition from a mom and pop franchisee shop to a recognized technological online retailer. As for Blockbuster video—well, that is another story entirely.

What happened to Blockbuster Video? Cloud-based internet rentals ate the VHS market for lunch. Netflix supplanted Blockbuster Video with a vengeance!

Not everything was available on demand in my early life. You actually had to sow before you reaped at that time. In large part because TES was not insidiously detouring everyone away from the actual experience of real life and the living of it. For instance, when it came to music back then, people still bought – and carefully played – records. Yes, I am talking about vinyls, people.

As a young boy with a record player, I had two types of records. There were the bigger rounder records we called thirty-threes (33s) and the smaller forty-five (45s) records that held fewer songs than the thirty-threes (33s).

Now, when a new record was about to come out, you would have to wait for the record to be released to stores. Then, you would have to physically drive to the store to procure said record, while making sure that you had a working record needle. That was key here too. Record needles often needed to be replaced, quite typically at the least convenient times.

The point is that there were no instantaneous downloads that would satisfy your immediate movie or music-based whims and other entertainment cravings back then. That was mere fantasy. Unimaginable fantasy. From the genre of science fiction, no less.

Get back to the basics in your life. See how TES has shackled you to the mentality of mediocrity, through life energy sapping distraction.

Come to know thyself. When you discover your true definite life purpose in the context of your overall life mission, your work becomes your joy. Your passion is to fulfill your definite life purpose. You shall become a living embodiment of excellence.

To obtain such a liberated position in life, you must first sow. Sow often. Sow early. Sow, sow, and sow.

To sow, you must first consciously plant the seeds necessary to ultimately win your freedom in this lifetime. This requires much time. Time for failures. Failures that lead one down the road of timeless treasure.

The very first thing that you must do to begin to walk a more exalted, and truly much more meaningful path than the average boy or man you see on the street, is to ditch your video game systems and other technological distractions. Take your time back.

Regain the helm of your mind, body, and spirit. Achieve greatness in your real life. Don't check out. Check in.

Once the video game shackle has been removed from your ankle, walk boldly further forward in the direction of achieving radical freedom in this lifetime. Get rid of your social media. Or, at least cut back on it. A lot.

Aside from video game addiction, social media addiction is the largest usurper of your valuable time, talent, and energy. Do not allow your most valuable assets, your time and your energy, to be siphoned off to fuel the insidiously capricious, and inherently noxious, collective world of social media distraction. Be smarter. Focus on the betterment of yourself, your family, your community, and your nation.

Focus on arete in all areas of your life. Become the gift to humanity that you were meant to be. You won't need to make a social media post. Others will be busily posting to social media about your achievements. Let them do the posting for you.

Avoiding the Instagram Trap

Social media is a time waster. Social media does not help you to better understand the world. In fact, it provides a false education to the multitudes. The miseducation of the marginalized. You will learn nothing about nothing and you will be outraged over everything. That is the very essence of social media frivolity.

The world is full of low information individuals desirous of all things free from the government or anywhere else for that matter. It is shameful. Don't be that individual.

Know that there is an absolute cost for any type of service or program, even the ones supposedly offered for free. Public goods don't come cheap, my friends. Even if the cost is your very dignity. Wake up. Put the phone away. See the oblivion of the masses.

People everywhere are constantly walking with their heads down, looking at their phones. Missing out on living altogether. Celebrating the inane lives of celebrities. Who cares what some nitwit pop star has to say about political theory?

It would be far better to gain insight from a political pundit. Would it not?

Why do we even care as a society what actors, musicians, or sports stars think about political philosophy, the re-founding of governmental regimes, and how we are to all live our lives both individually and collectively?

The vast majority of said Hollywood nincompoops vociferously espouse social and political views that are nothing short of opprobrious to everyday hard-working Americans. Far outside the mainstream. Are these nincompoop statements mere hyperbole? Is this all really just a spoof on reality? No such luck. They actually are serious. Worse yet, people take that crowd of halfwits seriously. Do not fall into that trap.

Think for yourself. Seek to fact check and verify any, and all, information that you learn about from independent legitimate sources of reliable information. Do not parrot the words of others without conducting your own investigation first.

Be knowledgeable. Being knowledgeable confers quite the advantage in a virtual sea of people who simply put just do not know that they do not know. Stop spending your time on social media reading about the greatness of others or lingering on your bed, getting fatter, less intellectually agile, and spiritually more bankrupt by the minute.

Wake up. Get rid of the social media addiction. Begin climbing your way up the ladder of success as defined and pursued by your own creative capacity. Awaken to your very own innate intelligence. Your achievements await.

When you do such great things that people make social media posts about the wonder, greatness, and gift of humanity that you embody, that will be thanks enough. Let your ego go. It is not really serving you anyway. Not in the long run at least, my friends. Egoistic ways of being will lead only toward the creation and circulation of narcissistic self-destructive energy, thinking, words, and behaviors within one's own human bodily vessel. Seriously, take a look around at your forebears. See the people in history that have exemplified the greatest qualities of human achievement and excellence in their lifetimes. Abraham Lincoln was one of those people.

The Abraham Lincoln Story

If there was a character attribute that encapsulated the very spirit of Abraham Lincoln, the sixteenth President of the United States of America, it was tenacious persistence. Lincoln served as President during a very pivotal time in American history, the American Civil War.

The American Civil War was not pretty, folks. It was a body-in-your-face killing type of war. A conflagration upon the nation. Lincoln had to make use of the countless lessons he had learned, from his myriad failures and defeats, to guide the Republic toward the direction of national healing and reunification. A coagulation in the wake of the bloody hostilities.

Lincoln lost eight elections prior to being elected President of the United States. History tells us that he won the Presidency right smack in the middle of one of the most politically and economically tumultuous times in the entire history of the Republic.

I use the term Republic for a reason. I choose my words carefully, my friends. The governing, and governance, structure of the federalist system of government in the United States is that of a Republic. Not a democracy.

A direct democracy entails one citizen, one vote. In a constitutional republic this is not the case. The United States would then be a constitutional republic as American citizens elect representatives to represent their ideas in the esteemed halls of the legislative assembly. So, therefore, your responsibility as an active, intelligent, and informed citizen is to understand for whom you are voting and why.

Many in the United States are waking up to the brokenness of our systems of governance. It is getting harder and harder to swallow the inanities emanating from our political, as well as administrative, caste overlords.

Due to our own collective gross negligence, we have allowed the big tech czars, as well as a few other billionaire vulture capitalists, to overtake the political processes. With the aid of the bought-and-paid-for politicians they finance and the deep state sinecure clinging bureaucrats who handle administration and enforcement, the foolproof plan to overrun our federal, state, and even local level electoral processes with cash has worked. What has happened to *We the People*?

The time for serious campaign finance reform, and strict term limits, is now.

It is also time to restore the notions of civility, and decency, to public office and to the public administration. Things have to change politically and socially in America. Or, we are going down collectively.

It is horrible out there today. People who disagree with you philosophically seem to have no compunction about going for the jugular. Destroying the career, reputation, and even life of the other, it is sick!

Good people simply do not want to run for higher office in this nefarious age of false allegations and character assassinations that are often driven by nothing more than political animus.

When you step back and look at the absurdity of American political and social culture today, it all becomes clear. This is all a big smokescreen designed to pit American against American. It's like a Trojan horse, if you will, inserted in our society to eat us alive from the inside out.

Both of the two major political parties are financed by many of the very same campaign finance contributors. Contributions from the very same corporations that are profiting immensely off the products that are making us all so very sick. With no real term limits in place, this elected caste of American wannabe royals, are able to stay in office for as long as they like. Doing darn near anything they like while they are in office. How does a Congress person, with a salary of a little more than one hundred thousand dollars annually, end up retired at the conclusion of a political career with millions in assets? You tell me.

Politicians throughout the history of our great nation have sacrificed to serve. Unlike the contemporary flock of way overpaid, completely underworked, sinecure seekers. Abraham Lincoln fell into that category of those who sacrificed immensely to serve the fledgling nation.

Abraham Lincoln shared little commonalities with the vast majority of the sycophants who masquerade themselves as politicians in this postmodern political hunger games. If good old Abe Lincoln were alive today, I bet my bottom dollar he would be calling for campaign finance reform. Damn straight. He would be calling for term limits as well.

As I sit here writing this manuscript today, there are candidates running for higher office that were first elected, to public office in the 1970s. Fifty some odd years of public life is way too long for anyone. I don't care how good their stories are! This is all such a shame. Wake up. See through it.

The endless funneling of corporate money into political campaign contributions needs to come to an abrupt and final end.

Study history. Learn about the inherently interesting characters who collectively founded the nation we know today.

There is much to be learned from such historical studies. You can make much better use of your time commuting to and from work or school, in waiting rooms and during other times of still patience, by carrying a physical book with you wherever you go.

Read it. Take notes in the book. Live in the book. Internalize the lessons of the book.

If you must lean on technology here a bit to get it done, so be it. Consider listening to books on audio.

Audio books are great in the car. Select nonfiction books about real world events and history in particular. The lessons you will learn, through the study of the life of Abraham Lincoln, are astounding. Not only does Lincoln encourage us to be self-learners, he also reminds us that having humble beginnings doesn't mean greatness can't still be achieved. He dares us to be courageous in the face of Goliath, and he calls us to be just as tenacious as he was.

Lincoln signed the Emancipation Proclamation in 1863, abolishing slavery, and tried uniting a broken country at the end of bloody war. He died before he could affect much reconciliation. He inspired a more enhanced global understanding of the concept of natural rights, universal and inalienable in the sense that they cannot be repealed by any human law.

Lincoln's presidency ushered in a new era of individual freedom and liberty for the nation and set the precedent for other countries. He is a great and historical example of what it means to be a divinely masculine man.

Better yet to learn from those who have come before you. Along those lines, think of all the people, especially the boys and men, you know with serious health problems, such as diabetes or high blood pressure. Both are strongly correlated with the consumption of CRAP Frankenfoods. Wake up.

Do not put garbage in your mouth and expect greatness to come out. Sow with your eating as well. Fill your human bodily vessel with organic, primarily plant-based food.

You will reap a harvest of excellence, in all areas of your own life.

Begin now. Stop eating acidic foods.

You Are What You Eat Exercise 3: Acidic Foods

In Lesson Two, I broke down the deleterious nature of what I refer to as CRAP foods. Let's get to the A in CRAP!

The third You Are What You Eat exercise focuses on acidic foods. Nearly all processed foods found in the supermarket and on convenience store shelves are processed acidic foods. Fast food is also highly acidic as well.

Stop buying CRAP Frankenfoods altogether. Stop consuming them in restaurants and in fast food drive thru lines. Begin today to get those excessive toxins out of your system.

When you put this book down, do a little bit of investigative journalistic research for yourself: What are acidic foods? What are some of the acidic foods that I should stop consuming at this time? What are some non-acidic foods that I should start consuming at this time?

Lean on your lentils in this lesson, my friends. Lentils, and other types of beans, are a strong source of low pH protein. Find organic, non-GMO lentils and beans to procure this week at the grocery store or market.

I like to place a bed of rice on a plate and cover it with black beans, pinto beans, and lentils. Lean on your lentils, gentlemen. They will take you far!

You can eat very well on the primarily plant-based path. It is far from the path of food deprivation. In fact, the eating of toxic CRAP Frankenfoods is the real culprit when it comes to nutritional deficiencies. There are plenty of seriously good muscle building proteins in plants, especially in spinach.

You will get leaner than you ever thought possible if you are serious about this effort and stick to the path. Eat sunlight foods in a primarily plant-based eating plan. Try to eat all of your meals at home. Pack all of your lunches and away meals if needed. I keep a cooler in my vehicle. It helps.

After three months of doing it this way, pull up your old bank statements. You will be shocked at how much money you have saved by cooking at home and packing away meals alone. There is a much greater benefit, of course. You will have treated your human bodily vessel as a temple.

In lieu of a steady stream of CRAP Frankenfoods, you will have put raw organic, non-GMO sunlight foods into your body, bringing forth light and expelling darkness. An addiction to CRAP Frankenfoods, ruled by those spoiled taste buds of yours, has nothing but ill health waiting for you.

In this age of ever-increasing pseudo-rebels, be a real rebel. Think for yourself. Eat sunlight foods.

Workout Exercise 3: Yoga

Yogic asana was originally developed for the purpose of awakening one's energy system.

Patanjali's Eightfold Path sought to catalyze unfettered energy passage through the body's energy channels.

Become a connoisseur of yoga studios. Yoga is not cheap. Do not throw away your hard-earned loot on a yoga studio where all the hotties in your area go and congregate. Yoga is not a place to pick up hotties.

Instead, choose a yoga practice that will push your limits. Remember to focus upon your health, your wealth, and your happiness. Partners, for whom you have immense attraction, are just on the other side of that equation, my friends. Tighten up.

Focus only on your yogic practice while on your mat. Off your yoga mat you can interact with women, and all other people, in a much more emotionally balanced and grounded way of being, demonstrating respect for self as well as the other.

Do not be fooled by the spiritual boutique clothing in the yoga studio windows, by the incense burning around tiny Buddha statues as you walk in, nor by the third-eye references included in the yoga instructor's final talk before ushering the class into restful dead man's pose, Shavasana. Namaste!

Most yoga teachers are really not at all spiritual. Yoga is, more often than not, a corporate sham where more emphasis is placed on the cost of your Lululemon yoga pants than on the progress made toward spiritual activation.

Most yoga studios tend to practice a form of yoga referred to as power yoga. Power yoga is influenced by intense aerobic exercise and is challenging in its own right.

I often encourage my students to practice some power yoga, but not to make power yoga the core of their practice. I steer my students to also practice hot hatha yoga instead. Specifically, the Bikram yoga series.

Now if power yoga is the only type of yoga available to you in your area, then go ahead, by all means, go and start a power yoga practice. If that is your situation, practice power yoga. Learn, and study, the Bikram yoga series online.

For those of you who are able to locate a Bikram yoga studio within an hour of your location, make plans to begin taking a Bikram Yoga class at least two to three days a week. I have practiced Bikram yoga through the years up to five or more times a week. Bikram yoga is the real deal.

There is little corporate malarkey going on at the Bikram yoga studios. The Bikram practice is serious as are its practitioners.

Generally, the Bikram yoga crowd is not as trendy as other types of yoga studios. Indeed, it is much more authentic.

Bikram yoga is hot. It is hard. It will hurt.

You will feel like you are going to die. You won't. You will leave the class invigorated after getting the best detoxification sweat of your entire life. It is so healthy for the mind and body.

Think of your body like a dish sponge. After a while, there comes a time when you have to wring out all the gross, dirty water and scum and reapply new soap so you can tackle your next dish. When was the last time you wrung yourself out so that you could have a fresh start? Bikram yoga will definitely wring you out.

So, go get yourself a good yoga mat and find a good Bikram studio with experienced teachers.

Take your yoga practice seriously. Arrive early at the Bikram studio, sign in, and try not to dilly dally chatting it up at the front desk. Place your towels on top of your mat and put your water bottle next to you in an easy to reach spot.

Before class, do not talk in the yoga room. Instead, lie on your mat focusing on your mission and purpose. Begin to silence your mind. Focus on your breathing. Slow the pace of your breath. Take deep breaths. Prepare thyself for the yoga practice ahead.

Go into your yogic practices with a seriousness of heart. That bold determination, which knows no bounds, that now defines who you are as a human being. Right here. Right now. Your stamp of arete placed upon all that you embody.

Again, you are not at the yoga studio to flirt. You are there to train your body, mind, and spirit. Take yourself seriously if you want the world to do the same.

When the class starts, listen to each and every word uttered by the instructor. Do exactly what the teacher says, when they say it, with no hesitation and to the best of your ability. Really do it. Give it your all.

Breathe through any limiting thoughts, or old memories, that come up in your stream of consciousness. Let all that go. Those old stories and narratives are simply not serving you on the path you walk now.

Focus on your breath. Focus on your listening. Focus on precisely following the directions from the yoga teacher. This is an exercise of focus that cultivates the habit of diligence and determination. It builds grit.

Often times, as the Bikram Yoga Series progresses, you may get winded as well as extremely overheated. That is normal. If that happens, just go to your knees and focus on getting back to slow deep inhalations and exhalations.

If need be, lie on your back in the supine position, face up. Again, focus on deep breaths. Unless you are pooping yourself or throwing up, do not leave the room. Just lying in Shavasana - a stillness asana that is still very much an asana - and sweating provides great health benefits. It sure helps me on days when I am completely wiped at the end of class.

Do what you can do. It is called a practice for that reason!

None of your yoga practices are going to be perfect. Ignore the fancy pretzel poses people rave about on Instagram. Focus upon your own yoking mind, body, and spirit. Focus on the advancement of your own spiritual evolution in this lifetime. Focus on activating and walking the path to awaken divinity within your own human bodily vessel.

Rid yourself of any mental roadblocks. How are distractions useful or in any way appropriate for your physical, emotional, or spiritual advancement? They are not.

Aim to be the second teacher in the yoga room. From your own mat, humble yourself and follow along energetically so you can encourage your classmates to do the same. Help drive the entire class forward by being a person others can look to for guidance and encouragement. Radiate motivational energy when you are in the yoga studio.

It will be hot. It will hurt. You will hate it. Do it anyway. It will change your life for the better in the long run, my friends. Now on to Lesson Three's Meditational Exercise.

Meditation Exercise Three: Yellow

Begin Meditation Exercise Three with the same pranayama breathing you started the first two meditation exercises with.

As you continue this self-scan of a meditative exercise, place your attention now to the yellow energy center located just above your belly button. This energy center is associated with the deadly sin of avarice, or greed. It is also associated with the concomitant virtue of charity. If you traverse up from the low C note where we started at the bottom red chakra, you will find that the yellow energy center is three up from the bottom. 1, 2, 3. C, D, E. Sing the E note out loud or try to hear it in your head.

Either way, feel the energy moving up the spinal highway as you vibrate those intonations. Feel the vibration of the E note in your solar plexus.

Now, depending on your present circumstance, either audibly or inaudibly vibrate the low C note, feeling the red energy vibrate in your groin area. Move up the scale to the D note, noticing the vibratory energy racing up, feeling your orange energy center just below the belly button. Move that energy up into your yellow energy center, vibrating your navel region and setting an intention for balance and harmony in your life experiences with both avarice and charity. How does balance and harmony apply to avarice and charity you may ask?

Consider this. You do not want to be the Grinch. Nobody seems to like the Grinch. Apparently, his heart is three sizes too small.

Yet, you also do not want to be known as the needy pushover who ends up giving all his time, money, and precious, priceless energy to others. There is a middle pillar way of being associated with this yellow energy center as there was with the bottom two red and orange centers.

That middle pillar path entails thoughtfully considering how charitable an individual wants to be and why. Once an individual decides how they want to allocate their resources through the development of a budget, it is done.

That individual will not have to cave into the pressures of others or the media programming. That individual gives liberally if they choose to do so or not.

Knowing that there is truth in the notion of what you give is returned back to you, it is up to each individual to decide how to live their own financial lives.

In this part of the meditation, enlarge that yellow energy circle from the size of a golf ball up to the size of an orange. Slowly pump your energy circle, treating it like a balloon, until it reaches the size of a basketball. Imagine yourself as the sun, as a warm ball of energy, spreading warmth and light to everything around you. Grow it again now, adding more and more yellow energy until it encompasses your entire body.

Now decrease your internal vibration and reduce the size of the yellow ball energy back down to the size of a basketball, then to the size of the orange, and finally take the yellow energy center all the way back down to the size of the golf ball. Ask to be shown the middle pillar path in the greed and charity areas of your life.

If you are feeling taken advantage of by others, do practice this yellow sunshine meditation thoroughly with care. Perhaps your default energetic level radiance is encapsulating your entire body with the radiance that you are the savior figure. Ready to swoop in and save the day!

Yet, afterwards you develop a strong resentment against those people you swooped in originally to help in the first place. In your yellow sunlight meditation, reduce the sphere down to the size of a golf ball sphere. Send out the vibration that you are a street smart, savvy, no cow pie type of individual who shall not be manipulated or taken advantage of in any way, manner, shape, or form.

Exude the energy of aware competence. Then, on your own time and at your discretion only you will have the capacity to truly dole out the type of help that you consciously have decided, upon your own terms, to share with humanity at this time.

Your time is your most precious resource. It is one of the few things that you just cannot simply buy more of.

Manage your time wisely and you will enter the esteemed halls of excellence in your field, making a mark on the world in this lifetime! Manage your time poorly, and you will be soon forgotten at the end of your existence of suffering in the malaise of the mediocre mentality. Onto the time management exercise.

The Time Management Exercise

This is the third of seven exercises that will allow you to apply what you have learned so far in real-world decision-making applications. For this exercise, you will need a pencil and paper.

Sit down in a comfortable spot. Commit to being there for at least an hour's worth of analysis. Turn off your phone to remove distraction.

Take out one sheet of paper. Make seven columns, one for each day of the week. Sunday, Monday, Tuesday and so on.

Now make several rows and label them Work, Sleep, TV, Video Games, Web Surfing, Watching YouTube, Working Out, etc. until you have a good amount of significant time-consuming activities you do on a weekly basis written down.

Just to give you a little insight into how this time management exercise works, you are going to be accountable for determining how you spent the twenty-four hours of each day last week.

For you, it might go something like this:

On Monday, you could have worked for six hours and slept for nine. Wait, what else did you do on Monday of last week? There are still nine hours unaccounted for.

Oh yes, you remember now. Last Monday you got that new video game you've been wanting after work and played it for four hours. That still leaves five hours unaccounted for.

Yes, you remember watching YouTube. You don't seem to remember what you watched. Or how that content could have helped you at all.

Still, you remember watching videos for about two hours before bed. Yet, there are still three hours unaccounted for.

Yes, get this specific with this exercise.

Often, it is only when we see how our time is managed, written down in blocks in front of us, that we ever truly register just how much of our valuable precious time here on Earth we are frittering away. As if we could all add more sand to the bottle. We cannot, folks. Take this exercise seriously. Wake up to how you are managing, or mismanaging, your own time.

Yes, yes, and yes, now you remember! You spent those other three hours last Monday fighting with your girlfriend. She was upset because a girl you used to like back in second grade, has come to work at your company. She is now serving as a work project team member.

The relationship is strictly professional. You are serious about your romantic relationship. Your second-grade fling has a fiancé. Moreover, she hasn't shown the least bit of interest in you. Other than a few light-hearted jabs here and there.

Still, your girlfriend insisted that something more must be going on. She felt it in her gut. As you recall now, she sent you a rude text. Then, you had to call her to talk her off the cliff. She hung up multiple times to ensue a call back from you, asking her to please not hang up on you again.

Finally, after three hours of that, she agreed that you love only her and that she should just let it go. That was the third time in the last two weeks she has tied up your time over nothing.

The morning after the fight, you woke up exhausted. You were late to work. You got a speeding ticket smack dab in the middle of mid-morning traffic. You can't help but surmise that you carried forth some of your girlfriend's negative energy right into that next day speeding ticket. Bingo. We have a winner, folks.

That is the exact point of this exercise, my friends. Map out the time drains in your life. Eliminate them accordingly.

Don't stop there. Keep going through every day of last week. You may become quite amazed at what you discover. It is often far easier to see how you are spending your time from the thirty-thousand-foot perspective, or the bird's-eye view. Here is a real-world case study in time management.

A young male undergraduate college student participant, at one of my recent workshops, discovered he was playing a popular video game forty-two hours a week. He worked ten hours that same week (it was a part-time), and he was simultaneously taking twelve credit hours at his college that semester.

Upon seeing the numbers on his sheet of paper, it was as if the young man's light bulb came on above his head, as you might see in cartoons. His eyes grew big as he tried to justify the expenditure of his own time mentally, before proffering response.

I asked the young man directly why he was spending so much of his precious time playing video games. Those games were not going to bring him health, wealth, or any real, sustained happiness in this lifetime.

The young man could clearly see the problem from the thirty-thousand-foot perspective. What a difference a change in perspective makes! Prior to this analysis, he couldn't see the whole of the forest from his place on the ground. He especially couldn't see what was happening when it came to the management of his own time.

Harken back now to the information I shared with you earlier on in this chapter regarding personal strategic life planning (PSLP). Think about what you want to achieve in this lifetime. See the initial time management sheet that you completed for this exercise through a new set of lenses.

How is your own time mismanagement holding you back from creating the life of your dreams wherein you will live on your own terms?

It really appears to be egregious in nature from the macro view. See yourself from that elevated position and vantage point. Once you truly begin to see how quickly those wasted hours have accumulated and coalesced, you'll want to start spending your time more efficiently, my friends.

Just how many hours are you frittering away playing video games, surfing social media, and getting dragged into the time-killing and energy-draining melodramas of others? How much of your valuable time is spent playing the side characters in someone else's mental play? See where you are mismanaging your time.

Now you are going to make a second time management sheet.

Structure it the same way you structured the first one. This time put down how you want to be spending the twenty-four hours of the day. Try to make a schedule out of it you will stick to, including going to bed on time no matter what type of drama your girlfriend is foisting upon the world this evening, to achieve the life of your wildest dreams. This is your new sow schedule.

Do not deviate from it. I advise you to let people know going forward that your time is valuable.

Juxtapose the list of what is being done with your time right now next to the second sheet and you should see significant differences in how the hours add up.

It is up to you. I won't be there. Your parents won't be there. Your coach won't be there. It is up to you to save your own life. Carefully decide, with the highest levels of definiteness of purpose, what you are going to do in this lifetime.

Consider your path carefully. Only you truly know what you are capable of and what you are here to do. Whatever it is that you decide to pursue, go after it with honor, dignity, and always, no matter what, see the job all the way through. Through to the end. Play with heart.

Lesson Four

Play With Heart

The fourth of the seven powerful fatherly lessons is titled Play With Heart. Nope! I am absolutely one hundred percent not referring to the big red Valentine's Day hearts. Not those ones. Wrong concept. The winner, folks, is diligence. Yes, diligence is playing with heart.

Diligence means putting careful persistent energy, work, and a mountain of concerted effort toward achieving the definite life purpose one has set out for themselves. Like most concepts in our dualistic reality, diligence has an opposing countering concept. That concept is sloth.

Sloth is the disinclination to put forth persistent energy, work, and concerted effort towards a predetermined life purpose. The very word sloth has a low frequency to it when the utterance passes one's lips. Does it not? Say it slowly aloud. Sloth.

Have you set forth strategic goals for your life? Do you have a personal strategic life plan? Are you attaining your goals through daily acts of self-motivated, self-disciplined diligence?

Or, would the low vibrational term sloth be a much more apt description of your current state of affairs regarding your advancement, and execution, of your personal strategic life plan? The key is to be honest with yourself.

Do you even know what it is that you actually want in your life?

Seriously. Contemplate that for a minute or two.

If not, figure that out. If you do not know the answer to that question, how are you going to get to your desired endgame? The answer is you won't.

If you have developed a definite life purpose in the overall context of your life mission, have you put those ideas down pen to paper? Have you developed a PSLP? Are you pursuing it with due diligence? Are you playing with heart in all areas of your life, both big and small? Let's unpack this concept a bit.

What comes to your mind when you hear the phrase "playing with heart?" Diligence should come to mind. Think of a great athlete, who has outperformed the field, as having played with heart.

On the football field sidelines, it is common to hear "that kid has heart" after a stellar gridiron performance. Referring to a player who has through deliberate due diligence, performed at the highest possible levels of greatness on the playing field. The concept playing with heart has real-world application. Off the sports playing field as well.

In the game of life, playing with heart simply connotes being present. Being at your very best. Training your mind, body, and spirit as you walk through the adventure of life in your human bodily vessel.

You are either living authentically, or you are not.

In the quest for true and authentic living, taking a personal inventory of one's relationships, activities, and habits is an utmost necessity. That is because you cannot really, in all fullness, attain your highest levels of serenity, peace, joy, happiness, and sheer unadulterated love of your craft in a job you hate. Now, now, now. Don't go off and quit your job half-cocked. Just because of a sentence you read in this book. Slow your roll.

Instead, wake up in your mind. Keep your mouth shut all the while. Knowing, and remaining silent is tough sledding at first. Once you get used to the practice, the joyous liberation from the need to reactively argue with others is quite the internal refuge apart from the suffering of the world around you.

Going forward, only make decisions that promote your own health, wealth, and happiness. Become less reactive. Much less reactive. Be much more strategically focused. Be more proactive. Much more proactive. Laser focused. If you are in transition from your current job, it should be done professionally. With the utmost respect to the previous employer, you gracefully exit stage left. Conduct yourself as a divinely masculine gentleman in all of your life interactions going forward from this breath.

A guy you know named Jonathan just up and quit his job. Throwing his fast-food apron at the manager. Blazing out of the restaurant door, one final time. Serenading the customers with a barrage of obscenities. He made his final exit. Is that really the reputation you want to have in your community? One of a hothead? A man-child with the emotional control of a baby? Do the right thing in all situations. It will bring you much more peace than shortcutting the processes due to your inherent fear, indolence, and hubris.

Prior to offering your current employer your two weeks' notice going forward, you should have a better job secured. All of this analysis should be done prior to submitting your resignation of course. The key here is not to make any sudden moves. Remember now the old adage. If you fail to plan, you plan to fail.

Think, analyze, plan. This is an exciting time of alchemical transformation in your life. New possibilities and situations are just around the corner on the horizon, my friends. Think of yourself as a diamond in the rough. You are refining yourself.

Why is a diamond valuable anyway? Diamonds can cut glass. Women seem to like them. According to the radio commercial, diamonds have differing cuts, colors, and varying levels of opaqueness and clarity.

Yet, if there were fifty other such similar diamonds on the same table in front of you, none of those qualities, or characteristics, would make the diamond valuable at all. Diamonds are only valuable, my friends, due to scarcity.

An awakened human being is far rarer than any diamond you will ever find. Hence, far more valuable. What is a diamond anyway, folks? A diamond is merely coal. Coal that has been alchemically transmuted through the application of extreme heat and pressure.

What are you willing to do to release your inner diamond? Are you ready for the extreme heat and pressure that will be coming your way? You can be. But first you must rid yourself of any, and all, unnecessary distractions. It is time now for you to get to work on you. The elimination of myriad distractions must transpire to allow you to laser focus on the achievement of your definite life purpose.

The biggest culprit in the area of the myriad distractions is the video game trap.

Avoiding the Video Game Trap

A common question, asked of me from my younger students, is what types of video games did I play as a kid? With fond memories, I tell no lie. I was privileged growing up in the era of the first video game systems. The first video game system that most people had in their homes was the Atari 2600. My family had one.

We played games like Pong, Space Invaders, Pac Man, and Breakout. Video games were quite the novelty back in that last bastion of the pre-digital age. Kids were able to play video games if they had good grades, if their homework was done, and after they had completed their chores.

Assuming a kid wasn't on some type of grounding or restriction, on an average school night, you might have been able to squeeze in thirty-minutes of video game play in those days. Why only thirty-minutes?

Well, for my younger readers, let me provide a bit of education here.

There was typically only one television set in average American homes in that day. Back in those days, the video game system was most typically attached to the only television in the house. The television set was the only video game monitor we had at the time.

Where was the only television in the house physically located? In the living room, of course. Imagine this: You have completed your homework. You are furiously playing video games, glancing up at the clock and knowing your time was extremely limited.

You can do the math here yourself. When your mom or dad was ready to watch the six o'clock news, your goose was cooked. Turn off the video games. Let the adults watch the adult programming. Having one television set in the entire domicile really limited gaming time for the youth of my day. Yet, that was not necessarily a bad thing. We should look into getting back to that way of being.

Yes, we played video games in my childhood. Yet, the video games of my youth were not free access all the time. There were healthy limits placed on gaming at that time. There are no such healthy gaming limits today. Therefore, you should impose such limitations on yourself.

Without your time being usurped, swirling down the drain of a video game addiction rabbit hole, you may just surprise yourself with what you can learn, do, and become. When you redirect your energies in a more positive and fruitful life direction, miraculous transformations replete with myriad blessings of health, wealth, and happiness, manifest in one's life. Usually in short order.

Stop the bleeding right now. Stop pouring out your precious energy and time. Get rid of your video game system. Learn to do real life.

Take a serious look at the number of hours that you are spending in the world of video game addictive distraction each week. It is a big-time waste of time guys.

Add up the number of video game hours that you are sending circling down the drain. Consider the reallocation of those hours to cleaning up your health, getting into terrific physical shape, and becoming the best student or worker at your job possible. Bringing abundance, as well as tremendous value, to everything and everyone you contact in your radiance.

In addition to getting rid of your video game system immediately - like yesterday, gentlemen - take the opportunity straight away to literally unplug from your devices. Often and a lot.

Do not let your life center around your phone. Wake up. Focus on the real world and what is happening with it. There is nothing wrong with stowing your phone in your car, or backpack, and walking without a phone in your hand twenty-four seven. Give it a try.

Take care to go places without your phone. See the world around you. Figure out your definite life purpose in the overall context of your life mission. The area that you will excel at beyond measure. Look forward to achieving what very few have ever found in this lifetime: absolute unadulterated freedom.

Put this book down immediately.

Walk over to the gaming unit. Unplug it from the wall. Place it in a box in your closet space. If others, such as siblings, are co-owners of the video game system, i.e. it is a community box, then take no such action.

Just walk away from the unit. Refuse to excessively think about it. You have too much work to do on yourself, in the furtherance of the creation of the greatest life you can manifest on the horizon, to be hogtied to that idiot box.

Don't game your heart gift. When you game your heart gift, you game yourself. Video game time diminishes significantly the heart gift that you should be bequeathing to humanity. Your so-called "video game achievements" are illusory. They only serve to reduce your desire to achieve real goals with real people in the real world. Level up in real life. It is far better to wake up in the video game of real-life than to watch it from the sidelines through the distorted blurry lens of electronic distraction.

Finally, exhaustive video game playing stultifies one's innate communicative intelligence. Thus, hampering intuitive knowing. Rendering one a literal fish out of water when it comes to your Spidey-senses, my friends. Making you vulnerable to physical, emotional, and spiritual attack during your interactions, with other human bodily vessels, off-line in the actual real-world. Keep your head on a swivel, folks. The most dangerous threat to your own existence, aside from the CRAP Frankenfoods that you are consuming each day, is of course other human bodily vessels. Watch them closely. You never quite know who is in charge in there.

Wake up. Seize the day. Create your definite life purpose in the overall context of your life mission. Pursue that definite life purpose with diligence.

Determine what your definite purpose in this life is and how it fits into your overall life mission. Spend time in careful reflection, creating a PSLP for yourself. Get rid of your video game system. Take your time back to achieve arete in all areas of your life and existence.

Carpe Diem: Definiteness of Purpose & Diligence

So many people are wandering the earth these days, staring down at their phones, in perpetual states of victimization, offended by the innocuous.

Unperturbed by the serious threats facing the United States today. Oblivious to all that is important. Always on the lookout for the external expert to tell them what to do, when to do it, and why. Groupthink has risen stratospherically. Concomitantly, free-thinking individualism is on the wane. Wake up, my friends. Do not fall into what German philosopher Friedrich Nietzsche referred to as the "autonomous herd."

The majority of digital era people have numerous distractions, very low levels of diligence, with little or no real understanding of their definite life purpose in the context of their overall life mission. Do not be like the vast majority of people.

Instead, decide right here and now that you are going to cultivate arete in each and every aspect of your life being. Carpe Diem is Latin for "seize the day." Seize the day, in your own life and existence.

Your definite life purpose is the work that creates harmony within your cells, the work that fulfills you. When you find yourself thoroughly engaged in the work that brings both joy and serenity, despite the physical, psychological, emotional, and spiritual challenges the work brings, you will have created your definite life purpose.

It is always far better to take on the challenge of creating your definite life purpose head on as opposed to wandering through your life existence semi-blindly. There are many pitfalls out there awaiting the aimless perambulators of life. As many of you reading do well know!

Following others down paths not of your own creation or design will never bring true happiness. Do not follow the autonomous herd.

Most people just set out to make a lot of money. That approach rarely brings lasting happiness. Instead, set your course for greatness as delineated in your personal strategic life plan. Get to work on yourself.

Once you decide upon your definite life purpose, determine the steps that must be undertaken to achieve it.

Will you need to go back to school? Is additional training required? Could you apprentice under someone currently doing what you want to do and learn the requisite skills needed the old-fashioned way? The key here is not getting all bogged down in the details.

Instead, come to an understanding of what your definite life purpose in the overall context of your life mission is first and foremost. Through your due diligence, the details will present themselves in synchronistical fashion.

Keep this in mind, gentlemen. Close to the vest if you will. Look around society today. Nearly every other boy and man you see is waddling around in states of overweightness and obesity, looking down at his phone darn near twenty-four seven on autopilot.

The boy or man who manages to escape both the tyranny of the taste buds, as well as TES, will have a great conferred advantage in the current societal setting where no one at all seems to be paying attention.

It is really not at all difficult to become successful today. Put down the electronic distractions and create. Wake up. Seize what is already yours. Plan for success not failure.

You have all heard this popular old adage before: if you fail to plan, then you plan to fail. Once you have created your definite life purpose, fueled by your own disciplined, strong, and steady diligence, you simply cannot fail. Now, get to work.

Get to Work!

If you cannot even remotely begin to fathom the nature of the design of your definite life purpose and overall life mission as of yet, do not stress! That is all unimportant. Knowing that you do not know is all important. An honest appraisal leading to the understanding that this is work that you need to do is all it takes. That, my friends, is at least a starting place.

All the information you will need to trek the road ahead will be earned along the way, have faith. As you are undertaking the self-refinement work, catalyzing your path of arete in each and every aspect of your life, the totality of the entire picture will reveal itself to you. That, my friends, is the very nature of faith. Remember, faith without works is dead.

Strive to become the best you can be in your current roles in life. If you are a student, become an 'A' student. If you are a salesperson, become the best in the district. If you are a businessperson, strive to provide the market with the highest quality goods, products, or services imaginable, at a reasonable price, and you will be amazed at the successes that life has in store for you.

Meaningful work, centered upon the fulfillment of your definite life purpose, is hands down the most rewarding path undertaken at any time by anyone across the history of human existence. It can also be – when done earnestly and authentically it usually is – lucrative for the person pursing their definite life purpose with heart.

Your definite life purpose will be revealed to you only once you get present in your existing life. Right now, as it is today, do not run away from your problems. Run toward them. If you want to set the stage for a better tomorrow for yourself, strive for the attainment of excellence in all areas of your current life today.

The energies of excellence will provide new paths for you. Those new paths of excellence lead to even more powerful paths up ahead. That is just how it works, folks. There are no shortcuts. At least not ones you would really want to take. If, of course, you had all the information prior to the selling of your soul.

There is only one way out: through. If you want to reach the pinnacle of life excellence, then it is absolutely paramount that you start cultivating the energies of excellence in your current life. Right now, as it is today, without geographic relocation and without any dubious reservation whatsoever. Face yourself head on.

Stop looking longingly at the horizon for some fantasy Publisher's Clearinghouse Sweepstakes minivan to pull up outside your door. People are not coming over in a minivan to rush up to your door with balloons and huge check in hand to tell you that you have won five thousand dollars a week for the rest of your life. That is just simply not going to happen.

Get out of fantasy land, gentlemen. Great wealth is rarely conferred in such an arbitrary and capricious manner. You know that! That is why it is a fantasy. Stop engaging in fantasy land. Get present on your existing circumstances and conditions.

Getting present with your current state of affairs, creating excellence in all undertakings, quite often leads one directly toward the creation of one's definite life purpose and understanding of one's life mission. Getting present is the keystone concept here. Thinking of a man who is really present in both life and career, Will Smith comes to mind.

I was watching an interview with him recently where he provided high level analysis on how he was able to leave a loving, yet impoverished, childhood behind to manifest a tremendous career of musical and thespian excellence.

For my younger readers, Smith arrived on the scene in the 1980s, as "The Fresh Prince of Belair." Will Smith's sage words of advice rang true to me as he was describing the alchemy of human inner transformation through the practice of first sowing and then reaping. Smith's very life is evidence of tremendous manifestations of success.

As a child, Smith learned the art of sowing before expecting to reap a harvest. Keep your eyes on the prize. Know yourself. Know your personal strategic life plan well. You have the roadmap for success in your hands, folks. Work like hell.

Outwork, and subsequently outshine, any competitor the field has to offer. Be Rudy Ruettiger.

The Rudy Ruettiger Story

With every conceivable odd stacked against him, provincially raised and lacking innate academic talent, Rudy Ruettiger was able to transfer by way of junior college into the University of Notre Dame. Notre Dame is one of America's preeminent academic institutions with a quite storied football program.

Once matriculated, at the home of the Notre Dame Fighting Irish, Rudy longed to walk onto the storied Fighting Irish football team. In fact, playing for the Fighting Irish had been a lifelong dream for Ruettiger. A boyhood aspiration!

Standing a mere 5'6 and weighing a paltry 165 pounds, Ruettiger was the most unlikely gridiron hero indeed to ever don the golden helmet and navy blue jersey of the Notre Dame Fighting Irish. Not having the brawn or exceptional innate athletic talents of the scholarship recruited athletes, Rudy was able to make his way onto the practice team.

Ruettiger stayed on the practice team by playing with heart. Rudy showed up day in and day out playing the role of whatever opponent Notre Dame was to face the next upcoming Saturday. Ruettiger was like a crash test dummy, taking powerful hits from men often twice his size, as he helped the starter players prepare for the Saturday game upcoming.

Ruettiger was indefatigable. He would take a massive hit and get right back up. No matter what,

Ruettiger always played with heart. Rudy displayed tremendous service on the team.

Service that was rewarded through the fulfillment of his childhood dream in the end. At the end of Ruettiger's senior year season on the practice team, the players to whom Rudy had been of such service stepped up to return the favor. The first string starter players forced the coach's hand to allow Rudy to dress-out for the final game of the season.

Winning the game by large margin, Ruettiger unbelievably was put into the game in the waning seconds of his senior, and final, football season at the university. Immediately, on the first play in, Rudy sacked the opposing quarterback in the final moments of the game. The crowd went nuts.

Rudy's parents were in the stadium. His dreams had come true.

Rudy sowed. Rudy sowed. Rudy sowed again.

Rudy reaped. Rudy had heart. No doubt. Big heart.

YouTube his sack of the quarterback and watch the Rudy Ruettiger movie, entitled "Rudy." You will be glad you did.

Folks, it is all about what you bring into your life that will serve as the fundamental primary determinant of what you get out of life itself. You can be as diligent as Rudy Ruettiger, but if you are eating tons of CRAP Frankenfood, the uphill path just got a whole heck of a lot steeper, my friends.

Consequently, if you are eating an abundance of CRAP Frankenfood and wondering why you are not feeling at the top of your game, maybe it is time for some eating plan changes.

You are what you eat. Exercise 4 focuses on eating sunlight foods in lieu of CRAP Frankenfoods of the processed variety.

You Are What You Eat Exercise 4: Processed Foods

The fourth of the You Are What You Eat exercises focuses on processed foods. Processed foods are all the foods that have been altered in some way during preparation. Adding preservatives, sugars, and high fructose corn syrup!

Now, I am not Chicken Little over here, claiming an imminent disaster, but there must be moderation in all things. True, all processed foods are not going to kill you immediately. Yet, over time they most certainly will take a toll. It is a simple, well-known truism that most processed foods are laden with high levels of sugar, salt, and unhealthy fats.

Therefore, for your health, wealth, and happiness you should make concerted effort to avoid all processed CRAP Frankenfoods altogether. Begin today. Make a serious effort to begin eating as many sunlight foods, and as few processed foods as humanly possible.

There are many ways you can go about doing this on your own. You do not need to go see a nutritionist. Do not pour more money down the drain by buying a bunch of books on the topic. It is really quite simple, folks.

Go to the grocery store and set your sights on procuring some organic blueberries, blackberries, and bananas for breakfast.

Pack a lunch of organic spinach with raw mushrooms, onions, and cucumbers with a touch of vegan salad dressing or oils. You will definitely not be feeling the afternoon bloat.

In the evening, place a few organic sweet potato yams in the oven, baking them until the candy goo starts to emanate from the cracks in the skin. Cut up organic pears. Sear them lightly in a shallow frying pan base of coconut oil. Slow simmer some organic asparagus in another pan.

Mash the sweet potatoes down on a plate forming a base for your dinner dish, a delectable delight, with the asparagus resting atop. Sprinkling in pieces of pear to top the dish. Enjoy.

Those are just a few ideas for eating raw plant-based breakfast, lunch, and dinner. Do your own experimentation trying out all types of organic non-GMO fruits and vegetables.

Remember that the consumption of raw sunlight foods confers the energies of the earth to the human body vessel. We, in these human bodily vessels, are all of course, from the earth. We shall return to the earth as well, my friends, in good time.

So then, please tell me why are we filling ourselves with CRAP Frankenfoods while we are experiencing our time here on planet earth? It simply does not make sense. It is making us physically sick. Very sick.

Get off the diseased hamster wheel. Begin to eat only the highest vibrational sunlight foods that emanate from our Mother Earth.

Reject the CRAP Frankenfoods that have so limited your full life expression thus far.

Combining right thinking and right eating with right cardiovascular exercise, a solid foundation for the alchemical transformation of your life existence is poured.

Keep it simple. Eat sunlight foods. Do isometric exercises.

Workout Exercise 4: Isometric Exercises

Workout Exercise Four focuses on isometric exercises. Do a quick internet search for the phrase isometric exercise. Your search return will reveal a tsunami of workout gurus, medical clinics, and other health industrial complex related websites. All replete with ads geared to sell you both pharmaceutical goods as well as various other health consulting services.

Do not get caught up in any of that nonsense. The first mistake people make these days is that of over analysis. Ever seeking to find the newest fad, promoted by the hippest and most woke expert who can tell them what to do, how to do it, all without really ever explaining why.

How many times have you heard science has said to do this or that for health and weight loss? Wait. No. Pump the brakes. Another so-called study has just emerged refuting the claims of the former. Making a convincing case for taking a completely different route altogether.

We are all inundated with information overload before the conclusion of breakfast if we do not take the proper care to shield ourselves from that never-ending radiation of cacophonous chatter.

There is no need to overindulge in analysis here. No need to get an expert trainer. It is all intentionally confusing. You are your trainer. Trust your inner guidance and wisdom and move forth. First and foremost, with this, and with many other things in your life, remember to keep it simple, folks.

The second most common mistake I have seen people make with their workouts is the pigeonholing of themselves into some type of category or another. Usually due in large part to egoistic self and group-validating identity attachments.

There are so many overweight folks squeezing into those Lance Armstrong bike shorts, preparing placement of their very large derrieres upon a rather small seat for a prolonged ride at what looks to be an extremely awkward, forward-leaning angle. Wouldn't those portly riders do better to stop eating the CRAP Frankenfood that is bloating them out in the first place? Perhaps learning to walk and breathe before attempting to dress up like a world class cycler would help keep them from looking foolish as hell. Once they find a regimen that works for them that will make cycling easier, then, yeah, squeeze away. Cycling has a lot of health benefits.

CrossFit also seems like it would serve us all well. As far as yoga goes, remember it comes in a wide variety of genres and flavors, ranging from the cute little yoga studio that sells fake Buddha statues and the newest Lululemon leggings to the hard-core Bikram hot hatha studios where the real sweat is going down.

Those are just mere examples. Yet, doing any one of those three exercises does not really seem to serve the majority of the people who are investing large amounts of time, and might I add money, toward these endeavors.

No matter how much cycling, CrossFit, or yoga you do, nothing of any real substance will change in your life whatsoever as long as you are continuously still eating the very CRAP Frankenfood that has been thus far fueling your suffering.

Your workout starts in your kitchen. Period. Listen to the needs of your human bodily vessel. Variation is the true key to building muscle strength, symmetry, and majesty.

I encourage you to follow the path of variation within your exercise routine. Also make sure you are allowing yourself time to rest.

Personally, I like to take one day off from exercise each week. The other six days a week I walk, practice yoga, swim, and do outdoor workouts at the park. I also like to work in isometric exercises.

Isometric Exercises involve the static contraction of muscle groups without detectible movement in the accompanying joints. The muscles experience resistance without lengthening.

For this reason, isometric exercise is often referred to as static strength training.

Scientific studies have shown that isometric exercises have both immense health enhancing, as well as strength building, benefits for the human bodily vessel. The term “isometric” is derived from the Greek words “Isos” (equal) and “metria” (measuring).

Isometric Exercise helps create an equal measuring body. Symmetry in the human bodily vessel is what you are seeking, my friends.

The three basic foundational Isometric Exercises for you to give a go are high to low planks, pull-ups, and the low squat maneuver. You know the one everyone likes to skip. From this day forward, do not skip leg workouts. Ever. In fact, do more of them.

High to low planks begin in a high plank, or pushup position. Come to your high push up. Then, you want to lower yourself one arm at a time, keeping your back straight and body parallel to the floor, until your elbows are on the floor and your chest is hovering just above the ground. Hold it, then push back up into high plank. Repeat eleven times or more. Just ensure perfect form before increasing the number.

Install a pull-up bar in your home or backyard, or locate a park to do pull-ups. Alternatively, a good tree branch will do. Hang from the pull-up bar. Become completely vertical, allowing your muscles to really stretch. Pull yourself straight up keeping your body completely straight and raise your chin above the pull-up bar. Then lower with control back down to your starting position. Repeat. Shoot for eleven repetitions here as well. Work up to it. Just ensure perfect form at all times.

Next, we squat. Perfect form here too, gentlemen. Every time. No exceptions.

Low squat begins in high squat. Bend your knees, lower your behind toward the ground, and look straight ahead at a point of focus. Engage the calves, the hamstrings, and the glutes to elevate the spine upwards as you exhale calmly and maintain your best form. Lower down to low squat and hold for eleven seconds. Then, raise up to high squat and hold for eleven seconds. Repeat eleven times or more. Just ensure perfect form.

Feel free to YouTube these exercises if you're more of a visual learner.

Get started with these three Isometric Exercises. Work on form. It is far better, in the long haul, to strengthen thy body. With perfect form, an increase in the number of exercise repetitions will come.

Now, let us focus upon the fourth of the Meditational Exercises. This green Meditational Exercise focuses on turning up the vibratory frequency of self-determination and diligence in your life.

Meditation Exercise 4: Green

Begin Meditative Exercise Four with the same deep, lung-stretching pranayama breathing technique that you have practiced at the beginning of the first three meditation lessons.

Move your attention now to the green energy located at the center of your heart. This green energy center is associated with the corresponding musical note of F. Om from the bottom low C note upward to the note of F. C, D, E, F. 1,2,3,4.

Practice it aloud, or in your head, once again. Do, re, me, fa. Om Fa, fa, fa. Feel it vibrating in your heart center and you will know that you are hitting the proper correct corresponding intonation and pitch.

People often think that the heart energy center must be associated with the verb love and the adjective loving. That is not at all the case. Actually, love is felt and experienced by the entirety of the physical human bodily vessel down to the cellular level, from the tips of the toes through the crown of the head.

One can use the human bodily vessel to experience many differing types of love.

In this exercise, we are focusing on the concept of diligence. The heart center's green energy is associated with the deadly sin of sloth and the concomitant sacred virtue of diligence.

Close your eyes. Whether on the floor, or seated in a chair, come into your mediation.

Thinking of balance in your green heart energy center, see the golf ball sphere grow as you increase the vibratory fuel with your powerful Om. Just like before, grow that energy center to the size of an orange. Then, to a basketball.

Now let the green energy engulf the entirety of your physical human bodily vessel. Feel the F note vibration at your heart center.

Ask for balance in your levels of life diligence. Set your levels of diligence on high during times of extreme push and work. Oppositely, turn down the diligence thermostat in times of rest. Rest is essential, my friends, when you are working on thyself.

Now reduce the green energy sphere down back down to the size of a basketball. Now to the size of an orange. Now take the green energy back down to the size of a golf ball vibrating at your heart center.

The purpose of these meditation exercises is to awaken your awareness of the various energy centers within your own human bodily vessel. With awareness comes the capacity for alterations.

Your attention goes where your energy flows.

With that written, let's move on to the examination of just how we can go about undertaking the breaking of screen addiction exercise in our own lives.

The Breaking of the Screen Addiction Exercise

We have all heard the phrase "screen addiction" thrown around quite often these days, yet there is veracity in its concept. Let's go ahead and just face facts here.

People are straight up addicted to their phones and other electronic devices. It is what it is. Our cell phones, in particular, have been allowed to become extensions of ourselves.

My grandfather often said that one day we will all be carrying a chip around in our hands. For identification and for purchases. He was right! The chip is literally in our hands. We are carrying it everywhere we go. Voluntarily no less!

What would you do if you left the house, got into your car or on your bicycle, set off down the road, and then all of a sudden came to the tire-screeching realization that you left your cell phone at home, unlocked on the kitchen table while other people are at home. You would come unglued.

I can hear the brakes locking up from here. Smell the tires burning as you undergo the sloppiest three-point turn of your life, heading straight away back to your house to retrieve the precious smart device.

These days, the electronic leash we call our phones is much more than just a mobile communication device. With internet access, today's smart devices have unlocked a gateway of potential for humanity. Over the last three decades, technology has crept into each and every area of our lives, often in highly intrusive fashion.

I am not advocating that you revert back to Luddite life. Do not eschew everything involving technological advancement. Technology is here and it's here to stay. There is really no disputing that, folks, or even trying to get around that fact.

Technology is not all bad. Not all bad at all. Screen addiction is not a requirement for proper usage of technological tools. Seek balance, my friends. Not digital device escapism. The key to breaking a screen addiction is for you to begin using technology instead of letting technology use you.

You use technology when you employ a navigational app to locate the nearest raw juice bar where you can get some good old fashioned sunlight juice. Technology uses you when you waste time watching videos, subconsciously taking in all the seen and unseen commercial cues, prompts, and other deleterious programming.

You use technology when you take online courses that advance your understanding of the world. Technology uses you when you, often unknowingly and unwittingly, volunteer your demographic and other valuable information to potential marketers.

You get the point, right? Use technology. Don't let technology use you.

Today, technology allows for interconnected global communications. Soon enough it will be interstellar or even intergalactic.

Technology has become such a big part of our lives. We must wake up to the notion of a much more nuanced, and altogether heathier, relationship with the technology that should be serving us.

The key is for you to learn to govern yourself when it comes to screen time. To keep your self-integrity high. Ensure that you are allocating sufficient time for the advancement of arete in your life. This is achieved through introspective self-analysis work, personal strategic life planning, and diligence in a person's ability to exercise governance over themselves. Self-governance is the singular most difficult area of mastery. Hence, it is the one you should be focusing upon most intently, my friends.

It is easy for a child to obey a parent blindly. Those children grow up to become adults who either never learn to think for themselves or level-headed intellectuals who know how to make decisions. Consequences antithetical to the furtherance of human liberation would ensue if all children grew up to be deluded groupthinkers. With quickness, whether we like it or not, all of us must communicate, cooperate, and collaborate with other human bodily vessel beings in the definite life purpose work.

Other human beings we encounter upon our life paths are at differing levels of spiritual evolution and understanding. Most, if not all, of them have largely fear-based, ego-driven challenges of their own that they are not working on.

How you react to such challenges, catalyzed through human interactions, is the key to the furtherance of your own health, wealth, and happiness. Remember this: it always is far better, and with much richer reward, to know thyself and to live in pursuance of your definite life purpose.

Keep in mind that you will need the assistance of other human beings to fulfill your definite life purpose. You must work with others.

How do you work with other human beings toward the furtherance of your definite life purpose while simultaneously avoiding the melodramas that interaction with other human bodily vessels so often entails?

There is one simple rule that will help you extricate yourself from most all of the various sticky situations with other human beings.

When it comes to your interactions, dealings, and affairs with other human beings on this floating space rock of ours, either serve or disengage.

Serve or disengage.

That one simple rule will help you to remain unentangled, free from many of the complications that people bring upon themselves these days in their interactions with others.

It is simple, my friends. Serve or disengage. Wasting time stewing upon what someone else said is utter frivolity. All of that misallocation of energy is simply a prolific waste of your time, mental energies, and heart force.

The simple, yet intricately profound, rule of serve or disengage will improve all of your dealings with your fellow humans. Applying this one simple rule in your life will reduce the drama you encounter on the daily in a highly-significant manner. Remember it. Follow it. Employ it. Do not throw pearls to the swine. That is simply just not worth your time.

Lesson Five

Serve or Disengage

The divinely masculine boy or man is aware of the inherent power of both thoughts and words to mold and shape reality. The divinely masculine boy or man is parsimonious with his words. Yet, he knows more words than nearly anyone.

As a general practice, with all of your reading going forward, look up any word in this book that you do not know. Look them up, then try to use those words in a sentence. If you look up and contextualize in a sentence a mere three words a day, you will learn a whopping one-thousand ninety-five new words a year. Knowledge is power, my friends.

Living by the rule to either serve or disengage, in all social situations and scenarios, is simply the most powerful implement found within your social toolkit. Remember this and repeat it in your head three times.

Do not throw pearls to the swine.

Throwing pearls to the swine is a prolifically irresponsible waste of your time. Become accountable for the stewardship of all of the time that you have left on earth school today. Your time and energies are immensely valuable. Don't waste any more of it on people pleasing. Living a double life of lies, largely out of your own fear of spiritual evolution and of the discomfort that comes with change, is really no way to go through life, gentlemen.

Living this one rule alone, to either serve or disengage at all times, will completely change your life for the better.

This simple way of being is to either serve others with your thoughts, words, deeds, and actions, or walk away from the situation physically, psychologically, and spiritually. If you have nothing nice, useful, or appropriate to say, then say nothing at all.

Serve the other human beings that you interact with at the time or disengage from said interactions altogether if you have nothing of positive substance to offer.

In short, when you remain mired in the quagmires of yesterday, the ever-repeating conversations you have with others will run circles in your mind, and you will have no peace.

Speculating on what you should have said or what someone meant by what they said is a time killer. Let that all go. The energy tentacles of those past conversations are still holding you back in those moments of conversational discomfort, dragging you down. Like pulling cinderblocks through sand, you are fueling the fires of your own destruction.

Long after another human being has forgotten the conversational incident altogether, you keep those fires of negativity enlivened within your own human bodily vessel through the fuel of resentment. It is draining you, folks. Avoid these issues in the first place.

Serve or disengage. Either think, do, or say something of service that will help the person and the situation or scenario or walk away. Keeping your thoughts, energies, and especially your words to yourself. If you don't have anything nice to say, walk away.

If you had to have one rule, and just one rule, to guide and govern your dealings with the 7.7 billion other humans occupying this planet, serve or disengage would be the go-to.

You should be of service, doing something of benefit for others, or you should disengage from the interaction altogether.

There is no debate about what to do when confronting challenging individuals or groups. You either think, speak, or act in service, or you walk.

Keep in mind that it is often what you do not allow yourself to become embroiled in that provides you with the cumulative competitive edge in all other areas of your life existence. Your time is precious. Energy is short. Do not throw pearls to the swine. Your short amount of time and your precious energy are meant to be spent on your own personal, intellectual, emotional, and spiritual growth and are too precious to waste on the affairs of others.

There is just no value high enough to place on the complete avoidance of problem situations from the get-go. Moreover, it is a simple rule in itself. It is in you already. No need to look for an external solution!

Unless you are being paid a handsome sum on a television talk show to fight out gladiator style, debating contentious issues with a fellow interlocutor, don't do it. Your time is valuable. Do not waste it on others.

Most of us, nearly all the time, fail to comprehend that we create the majority of our own suffering in life. Mostly by what we volunteer to get ourselves into in the first place. Now, don't get me wrong. There is injustice in the world.

That is an understatement, for sure.

Abused children, victims of genocide, and others, who suffer under the harsh hands of tyrants, did not volunteer for that suffering. Yet, in our daily lives most of us have quite the penchant for bringing big troubles to ourselves. Through careless loquacity most often.

It is through our gregarious need, often grounded in extreme neediness, that we feel so compelled to fulfill the urge to tell the world how we feel about everyone and everything. This often leads to the sticking of one's foot in one's mouth, usually at the most inconvenient moments.

These are dangerous times, gentlemen. Take a look around.

Countless numbers of men have lost their careers and positions. Many have undergone public shaming on the social media pillories of the day. Innumerable have been ostracized to the margins of society. Some of them never to be heard from again.

Apparently, there is little forgiveness left in this world today. A world bereft of forgiveness is quite the scary place indeed. Act as if you are being recorded at all times, you probably are.

Avoid any sexual harassment, sexual misconduct, and even the likes of sexual innuendo in all of your speech and writing. This includes texts, posts, and emails, gentlemen. You are hereby put on notice. Right here. Right now. If you do not, there will be consequences.

The chickens have surely come home to roost. Have they not, my friends? The egregious misconduct on the part of many named male celebrities, public officials, and other so-called stars, has caught up with many of them. Without question, anyone who commits such crimes should be held to account to the full extent of the law. Yet, also all must come to an understanding of the fact that we are living within the age of the war on men. The very concept of masculinity is being attacked in general. That too is a dangerous trend.

Nowadays, all of your words and actions are closely monitored and often memorialized on social media. It is in fact sage advice for you to watch what you say and do very closely. Others will be!

Remember that even the appearance of impropriety can be extremely damaging to both your personal and your professional lives. Even when you have done nothing wrong. There are people, in this new age of the war on men, who will have already decided that you are toxic prior to even meeting you. They will not need to know you at all whatsoever to make such preposterous and sexist diagnoses.

Do your best to avoid these people to the fullest extent possible. Limit your exposure to their toxicity.

The very negative toxicity that they are so brutally projecting onto you is probably a mere projection of their own self-loathing. Do not let such cretins get under your skin. If prolonged interaction is required, act as if you are being recorded. You probably are.

Remember to apply both Occam's razor and the power of parsimony of speech and text in your life going forward. Looking back a few years from now, you will sure be glad you did!

Applying Occam's Razor and The Power of Parsimony of Speech and Text

Today's world has become socially complicated. Times are a-changin', my friends. Quite rapidly, it seems, and not always for the better. These are politically charged times indeed, wherein groupthink and the mob mentality have gained momentum at the societal level, further suppressing the free-thinking individual.

Nowadays, given the political and societal complications involving the rules of political correctness, you really can't win for losing. You must constantly walk on eggshells just to ensure that you do not offend anyone unintentionally.

To hell with their microaggressions. Friends, there are just too many pitfalls in that clammy game for me. I am not playing anymore.

Today, I keep my conversations and interactions strictly professional while in public. Both at work and at play. Unless a person falls within my circle of trust, they really will not have the opportunity to get to know the real Matthew Lloyd Collins. I now protect myself from wolves. Develop like rules for your own life.

With the burgeoning popularity of notions of critical race theory, as well as the innate gender bias, as a boy or man, you really can't win for losing. You are either a sexist. Or a racist. Or both.

It matters little how you personally treat others, as you are often going to be assumed guilty of sexism and racism, nonetheless. By virtue of your levels of melanin and your plumbing alone!

Even when there is no supporting evidence whatsoever.

Especially when there is no supporting evidence whatsoever.

Even if you are a gentleman in every respect when it comes to your treatment of girls and women in your life, some folks will just take you as a toxic male anyway. There is only one solution for you.

Exercise parsimony in both your speech and writing. Yes, this includes text messaging and social media posting as well!

Be professional in all of your interactions, all the time.

Let your guard down only with a selected few inner-circle folks who have come to earn your trust through loyal dedication. This is simply your best defense in a toxic world that will project its venom against you and make you a male scapegoat, the one to take the blame for the amalgamation of societal problems. Just because you have the wrong melanin levels or the wrong plumbing. How ludicrous is that by the way?

We have lost our way in America today, my friends. No longer are our values centered squarely upon the natural rights of the individual predicated upon the notions of both due process and the presumption of innocence. No, those days are gone. Today, they focus instead squarely centered upon toxic tribalism where your race, sex, and sexual orientation are more important than the content of your character. It is sad. If this collective delusionary focus on identify politics continues unabated, it will be the ruination of America. We in the United States must now get back to the basics. We must break the chokehold placed upon us by the postmodern theories of the academic left that have seeped into popular culture, like fentanyl, with much more devastating consequences. Make use of Occam's razor, my friends.

Occam's razor holds that the simplest solution is most likely the most useful one. Obey Occam's razor. You don't have to look far to see guys who, usually through their words and deeds, have found themselves out of careers while sustaining massive defamatory hits to their personal lives. The war on men is real. It is happening today all around us. The sins of our fathers now beset us in our time. Whether we, as individuals, are cut from the same cloth as the misogynists of yesteryear matters not.

There is no presumption of innocence today for men and boys. There is only a presumption of toxicity. So, men and boys today must take measures to protect themselves from unwarranted allegations and accusations. The best protection plan, to guard against such, is to dutifully follow the lesson to either serve or disengage.

Think what you like. However, take great caution with whom you express your inner thoughts.

If you don't have to say it, don't say it. Never write it. Whatever you do, think three times critically before your press send on a post, email, or text. Especially those composed in a time of emotional upheaval, angst, or what is most often illusory delusional righteous indignation.

First and foremost, respect yourself, as well as the rights of all others, at all times.

Serve or disengage at all times. Always. If you do that alone, you will find that you will avoid the majority of life's social challenges and energy-sapping, melodramatic upheavals.

Think for yourself. Keep those thoughts to yourself. Eschew groupthink and stop parroting others!

Eschew Groupthink & Stop Parroting Others!

We live in the age of copycat killers and Instagram frauds. Principled decision making, thinking for oneself, and displaying the courage of your convictions for the whole world to see is on the wane. Toxic tribalism, through mob rule collectivism, is waxing hard. If you simply just go with the group, then you abdicate the responsibility of determining what is right for you and the collective needs of your fellow citizens in society.

While you are off anesthetizing your intellectual, emotional, and spiritual senses, playing video games into a thumb-blistering, stultification stupor, others will decide what to do with your time and talent. There will be no need for your input. No need, whatsoever.

Wake up, gentlemen. It is time to standup for yourselves. At the core of the most insidious groupthink narratives being tossed around in everyday common vernacular these days, is the claim that all of masculinity is congenitally toxic.

That is a bold-faced lie. Not all of masculinity is toxic, not even close!

Begin to awaken to the numerous other toxic lies brought to you today, courtesy of the attack on individualism in general, masculine individuality in particular.

Strong masculine figures are most threatening to the toxic, tribalistic mob that has come to power in the United States today. That very same mob is busily conjuring up the new social rules that all of us will be forced to acknowledge, passively accept, and live and abide by.

Or, we can face the tidal waves of opprobrium, littered with hate-filled rhetoric and emanating from any number of politically-motivated lunatics all about us today. They are anti-individualistic enforcers of toxic tribalism. They are the ones who no longer give any credence to the rights of their fellow citizens to peacefully assemble. Gone be all of our first amendment rights.

See the lunacy of the world around you. Isolate, and insulate, yourself from the toxic radiation of such. Your best hope for self-protection, in these inherently dangerous times for boys and men, is to start thinking for yourself. Awaken to your own groupthink programming and make necessary self-corrections. Avoid the habit of parroting the words of others in totality.

Take time in your day to stop talking.

Quell your mental chatter as well.

Begin listening to the words of others instead. You may be surprised what you hear. If you undertake this exercise with any seriousness and focus, you will inevitably find that people say the same things repeatedly without knowing it. I often refer to this as parroting.

From the time that we were small children, we all started parroting the words of others. That is how we learned to talk. Once we could talk and began to think for ourselves, we should have been further instructed to let go of that parroting approach so we could cultivate our own inner awareness and critical thinking capacity, expressing such through insightful and cleanly-efficient speech and writing instead. Now we all know that is really not at all how that goes. Yet, it could go down that way for you, if you begin the work of self-refinement.

What you will hear during your listening experiment is people parroting what they have heard others saying in the past, verifying my parroting theory in your empirical experimentation. In general, other human bodily vessels are chatterboxes of the parroting variety whose motivated self-interest will outweigh any real sense of justice nine times out of ten. Beware of other human bodily vessels. They are dangerous.

Outside of your vetted social circles, professional it is, gentlemen.

Wake up. Become aware of how you fall into the groupthink trap. Be mindful of your thoughts. Your thoughts manifest actions and your actions have very real consequences in very real time.

Remember, for the love of everything righteous and holy, to never send threatening emails, posts, or texts to anyone at any time for any reason. Pay attention. This is serious business, gentlemen. Treat it as such!

Never Send Threatening Emails, Posts, or Texts

Do not ever send threatening emails to anyone, anytime, for any reason. Just don't. At the time of this book's writing, the twenty-four seven cable news loop reports are going on and on about some teenaged boy recently arrested for allegedly seeking a hitman on Instagram to assassinate a staff member at his high school. Don't post threatening statements to social media. It will not be perceived as a joke. It won't. So, just don't.

Concurrently, an incredibly talented National Football League (NFL) star player was fired for allegedly sending inappropriate text messages. Others have lost their lucrative sports careers for social media issues, threats, and other inappropriate, less than useful, postings. Structure your life so that you have no need to threaten anyone. If threatening must be done to protect your interests, allow your attorneys to undertake that fight. Protect yourself knowing that your own emotional instability, and lack of control, is really your own worst enemy. Nine times out of ten, it is.

Do not express yourself digitally wherein the context of your messaging can be misunderstood, or even boldly distorted, after the fact. Text message vigilantism on your part, even if you are in the right, can cost you your career. Worse yet, it can land you in the slammer.

Here is a little hint. Think whatever you like, but be cautious in the manner that you share said radical thoughts. Keep your emotional responses to life and the living of it to yourself as much as possible. I am not saying to bottle up your emotions, to stew on them internally until you need antacid relief, not even close. Find a mentor, preferably an older man with whom you share commonalities, to talk about these issues within a setting of mutual respect and clear, straight forward trust. Do not throw pearls to the swine, my friends. What I am advocating is for you to begin working on strategic taciturnity.

Strategic taciturnity entails not reacting to social stimuli in an uncontrolled manner. Exercising strategic taciturnity means not yelling back at your girlfriend when she accuses you of some nonsense. Learn to control your emotions. It is truly your only hope. Instead of returning high-volume verbal fire in her direction, stop and allow your mind to quiet. Go back to the meditation exercises learned within the lessons in this book. Begin your low C Om. Feel the swirling red energy in your loins grounding you down.

Begin your pranayama breathing exercises knowing that reaction is a choice. You very well could also elect to save your energy and your precious breath and walk away from what could very well escalate to a domestic violence incident. You want no part of domestic violence. Govern yourself accordingly.

Realize that saying nothing and walking away, making use of strategic taciturnity, is your very best immediate option for staying out of the jackpot.

Consider a permanent walk away because you should not tolerate vicious, accusatory nonsense in your life going forward.

Plan quietly for the surprise departure, my friends. From this day forward, you elect to respect the rights of others. In parallel fashion, you project to the world that you will not tolerate the disrespect of yourself either for that matter. Henceforth, you teach people how to treat you!

Many of our relationships have grown into ones of the highly toxic variety. Often, you must change the nouns in your life. The people, the places, and the things. One step in the direction of this self-metamorphosis is to stop doing what you have always done and get to work on your own health, wealth, and happiness instead.

Consider finding more reliable people to talk to and develop relationships with both a confidant and a mentor. Develop relationships with trusted friends, who serve as allies, and guard your communications like a vault. Find mentors who will share their life experiences with you, providing you guidance and dependable sacred wisdom.

Communicate with these types of people often. They are your trusted sources for information deposit and withdrawal. Your private life is just that, your private life. Keep it that way.

Watch what you do and say at all times. Be judicious in your pronouncements and strategically taciturn in all of your dealings with other people both in in-person and online interactions.

Running your big mouth on social media has been the death kneel for many people's careers. Often times for their freedom as well. Put your ego aside. Focus on the real world. Achieve real goals, in real time, in the real world. Do not allow your life experience to be usurped by the envelopment of all of your emotional energies.

Liberate yourself. Wake up. Unplug. Start living. Beware your digital footprint. Social media is not furthering your health, wealth, and happiness. Just the opposite. Social media is a time killer. Jettison it. Repossess your time. It is yours. Social media is not a good source of useful information.

Misinformation abounds on social media sites. Seek information from peer-reviewed academic journals and trustworthy nonpartisan journalists who have a solid understanding of the political and economic models of Western civilization.

If knowledge is power, then misinformation, and disinformation, gleaned from pressing the social media button, is the quintessential path to the embodiment of disempowerment. Social media can be dangerous and deadly for your career.

How can something I posted ten years ago affect me now? Just ask a well-known comedian who did not get to host an award show because of a dangling digital footprint that reared its ugly head at the most inconvenient time.

Those decade old posts are hanging around out there in cyberspace, ripe on the vine just waiting to be discovered, and revisited, by future enemies seeking to tar and feather your character through ad hominem attack. People will try to destroy you, usually because of an insignificant disagreement you had regarding a socially-constructed issue. It is sick. Truly sick. Pay attention here, gentlemen, as this could happen to any of you.

Social media posts from yesteryear that didn't seem to offend anyone at all have a nasty habit of resurrecting themselves in current times wherein great offense can be taken. When this happens to you, your reputation will be defamed mercilessly. You may not be able to host the award show even after your apology tour. Beware your digital footprint. Just ask Carson King.

The Carson King Story

Carson King was a young man in his early twenties who absolutely loved himself some college football. Carson decorated a sign for College GameDay that asked people for beer money donations and it went viral online. The donations started pouring in. They kept pouring in. What started as a ruse prank gone viral, burgeoned into an internet sensation.

With the high dollar amounts floating in, King decided to donate the entire sum – which ended up being close to three million dollars – to a local children's hospital.

You would think that would have been the end of the story. A guy played a prank. The prank went viral. The enormous sum of money was bequeathed to charity. All is well that ends well. Right? There is no enemy to shoot there. Or, was there? This is just not a good time to be famous, folks.

As meddlesome people often do, in this age of unforgiveness, someone dug up an old tweet wherein Carson King, as a sixteen-year-old boy, had referenced a racially charged segment of a television show. What had gone from being a positive story with a good ending for all had to be sullied and made unnecessarily nasty. This is why we can't have nice things.

Carson King was forced to apologize for social media posts, made many years ago in his juvenile days, that simply were not reflective of the man that he had grown up to be. The man who gave the money to the children's hospital when he really did not have to do so.

Just know that these are very dangerous times in which we are living. Protect yourself by exercising strategic taciturnity outside of your vetted and highly-trusted circle of friends. Conduct yourself professionally at all times. Act as if you are being recorded at all times.

Beware your digital footprint. It will come back to bite you in the behind. Begin now to take great pains to immediately eliminate any digital footprint you could still have.

Minimize your social media presence going forward. Refocus, and reallocate, your life force toward the manifestation of the health, wealth, and happiness that you so desire in this lifetime. What good is all the money, and wealth, in the entire known multiverse if you cannot get out of bed to enjoy life? How important is having tons a money for someone who is too out of breath to climb up and down a flight of stairs?

It is time for you guys to redefine wealth in your heads. Come to the realization that your health is your wealth.

Let's face it. Without health there is no real wealth. This week, consider the advantages of primarily plant-based eating for the bringing about and manifestation of your overall health, wealth, and happiness.

You Are What You Eat Exercise 5: Introduction to Primarily Plant-Based Eating

The fifth You Are What You Eat exercise introduces the primarily plant-based eating plan.

As I have said before, I am in no way qualified enough to tell you what to eat or what not to eat. I can only share my experience, strength, and hope. I can testify, with full on veracity, as to what primarily plant-based eating has done for me.

At one point, I was nearly two hundred eighty pounds. I am only 5'11. I wore size thirty-eight waist pants. Today, I am one hundred eighty pounds and wear size thirty-two waist pants. I wore that same pant size in high school more than thirty some odd years ago now. How did I do it?

In this section, I will make a compelling case for the inclusion of sunlight foods in your eating plan.

It is well known in the scientific literature that eating fruits and vegetables is correlated with diabetes prevention, hypertension control, heart health, weight loss, fiber intake, vision health, and clear skin radiance. Conversely, it is also very well known that eating mostly processed meats and CRAP Frankenfood is strongly correlated with diabetes, high blood pressure, obesity, fiber deficiency, advanced age-related macular degeneration, and cruddy skin.

One would think that knowledge would have the power to stop people from consuming garbage, but it seems as if people are looking at the facts and ignoring them.

It's obvious that they are, otherwise the 75% of men in the West who are overweight or obese would not be. Boys are not too far behind! More and more boys and men are becoming more morbidly obese by the day.

We must stop this insanity.

Awaken now and begin to take responsibility for your own health, wealth, and happiness. Corporations offering pseudo-advice on how to be healthy simply do not have your best interests in mind, despite what their advertisements say. You, as a free thinking individual, must change your perception of the collective delusions that are no longer serving your highest interests whatsoever. Elect to forget everything that you think you know about food and eating. Develop an eating plan concept for yourself. Stick to a primarily plant-based eating plan.

Do you really think it is a good idea to eat processed, preservative-laden Frankenfoods that have been shipped to your house? Why is it that we are told it is okay to eat one thing, then, another study comes out and tells us it is actually not okay to eat that thing?

Do not believe everything you hear. Do your research and eat foods that will provide you with the vitamins and nutrients your body needs to function properly.

Eating plant-based sunlight foods is the best way to maintain your health. It's a way of consuming that focuses on inner healing.

That is not to say that you can never enjoy meats and other types of foods. That is entirely up to you.

Just understand that CRAP Frankenfoods are destroying the human body from the cellular level outward.

I also advise finding role models who follow the very same lifestyle I'm asking you to commit to. Not only do they help motivate you but they are also a great source of inspiration when it comes time to make note of what to buy and what meals you're going to want to eat.

Eliminating CRAP Frankenfoods from your diet will help you lose weight, improve your health, and save money.

Speaking of putting a little more money back in your pocket, I'm going to tell you a secret.

You do not have to spend hundreds of dollars on fancy gym attire and memberships to get in the best shape of your life.

An outdoor area large enough to work out in is a costless way of setting the foundation for your physical transformation. Let us get underway. Park workouts are up next!

Workout Exercise 5: Park Workouts

Workout Exercise Five focuses on park workouts. It is totally cool to use public park equipment for workout purposes if, and only if, you respect the park, the park's equipment, and the people around you.

A quick piece of advice. Don't, just don't, be the creepy guy who loiters at the park, especially near the playground. You are there to workout. Not to socialize, not to people watch, not to accidentally get called a pedophile.

There are many great benefits that come from turning the outdoors into your personal gym. Exercising outside has been proven to reduce stress, improve insomnia issues, lower blood pressure, and who can forget that it's totally free.

I begin my park workouts with some kind of cardiovascular warm-up. I personally like to walk for about a mile and a half. Remember that walking is one of the greatest exercises out there. Don't brush it off.

After your cardiovascular warm-up, take a few minutes to stretch yourself out. Really focus on stretching your calves, hamstrings, shoulders, neck, and everywhere else you hold a lot of tension. Don't forget your hips. Take a break from all distractions and connect with the earth beneath your feet.

After you stretch, you are going to want to execute some three to five exercises. These could include the three isometric exercises from before, but Bulgarian split lunges, elevated push-ups, or any kind of dip exercises are also good places to start. There are so many ideas online too, so have at it.

To make this new training more effective, high-intensity cardio interval exercises are the best way to finish your workout. This means you are going to want to save about ten minutes worth of energy for a killer cardio finisher. Anything from sprinting to jumping rope to burpees will serve as good exercises here. Plain old running also works just as well.

Remember to focus on perfecting the form of each exercise. Sloppy form won't yield the results you are aiming for. It will just make you tire faster and also make you look like a noob.

Remember also that workouts are a form of meditation. While you exercise, revisit your definite life purpose and take note of the steps you took that day to move you forward towards it. Unplug from your devices as well. Be fully present wherever you are.

While you exercise your human bodily vessel, try to also exercise kindness. Specifically towards yourself. Thank yourself for wanting to transform yourself into the best version of you. Appreciate how much hard work you are putting in to fix your current mindset. Compliment your body on how well it is performing the exercises.

And on that note, let us move on to Meditation Exercise Five.

Meditation Exercise 5: Blue

Begin Meditation Exercise Five with the pranayama breathing warm-up technique. Turn your attention now to the blue energy located at your throat. If you count – starting from the red energy center of the groin – the blue throat center is the fifth energy center up. This center is associated with the G note on the musical scale.

Go ahead and give it a try. Once again, you can choose whether you do this aloud or not. Traverse up the C scale and you will ascertain that the throat area is five steps up from where you started at your low C note red energy center. Alignment is important in life. Alignment between deed and word. Thoughts precede action. Even if we are obliviously unaware, and often blissfully so, of these formative processes.

An interwoven theme that pervades this book is that the vast majority of us create many of our own life struggles, problems, and challenges by allowing ourselves to atrophy physically, emotionally, and spiritually.

We impose these blockages on ourselves because our thinking and actions are out of alignment. The things we think are all consequential in nature and whether or not we allow them to negatively or positively influence our actions is up to us. If our car's tires need to be aligned, do you want to just think, "Eh, it will be fine," or are you going to be motivated to go to the mechanic and get them fixed? Think of yourself as a car that needs realignment. Yes, you work all right with unaligned tires, but you will work so much better with realigned ones.

Coming from a place of integrity does not mean that you are a pushover. Far from it. Create healthy thinking that will lead to alignment between your thoughts and actions. With this in mind, vibrate your fifth energy center G note to really awaken the energy in your throat center.

Envision your golf ball sized blue throat center's energy sphere enlarging as you increase the amplitude of the vibratory fuel you are providing through your audible or inaudible Om. Grow your blue throat vibration to the size of an orange. Now, to the size of a basketball.

Now go full force, as you have done four other times already in the past four exercises, and grow that blue energy sphere to encompass your entire human bodily vessel.

Ask for balance in the areas of wrath and forgiveness, and then decrease your energy sphere down to the size of a basketball once again. Now, to the size of an orange. Slow the frequency down now to the original golf ball size.

Balance in the area of the blue throat energy center has been achieved as you make the necessary changes to your bodily vessel in the pursuit of bettering yourself. Set the intention to serve or disengage.

Now, we are onto the Non-Reaction, Non-Attachment, Just Walk Away Exercise. This one is a dandy!

The Non-Reaction, Non-Attachment, Just Walk Away Exercise

This is the fifth of the seven exercises that will allow you to apply what you have learned in this book to real-world, decision-making situations. Here we go again with yet another exercise to sharpen your mind, embolden your spirit, and create a buffer that will protect you from the cold winds of suffering.

For all the conferred benefit that living out this exercise will bring you, it is surprisingly simple to understand conceptually. All the while, it is simultaneously the most difficult to master and articulate, especially if under duress.

This simple exercise asks you to evaluate situations and pull out your strategic silence card, slapping it down on the table and walking away, when the situation turns out to be hostile. It will ask you to decipher what your limits are so that you can walk away from situations that would encourage you to overreact a bit and probably leave you embarrassed after it is all over. That seems easy, you might be thinking. It is not.

Let me invite you to reflect on the last time that you were truly embarrassed publicly because you overreacted in some matter or another.

How many people were hurt by the things that you said or did in your overzealous reaction to the stimuli that presented themselves to you? How many hours did you waste stressing out over the outcome of that particular situation?

Has your wrath ever gotten the best of you? Where did all that rage lead? Good places? Probably not.

Get honest with yourself about how you react to situations that confront you on the daily. Are you proactively anticipating any issues before they arise in an attempt to avoid the need to be reactive?

Immediately start becoming aware of the social stimuli that make you irritated to the core and try to figure out why they do. Try to figure out what you can do about it.

First, make a vow to yourself to refrain from repeating the wrath mistakes you have made in the past. Raging out of control is no way to go through life. Temper down. Get strategic. Carry out your strategies through smart tactics to ensure that you come to the ends that you so desire to manifest in this lifetime. That, my friends, will unabashedly prove to be the far better way.

The next time that you are confronted by social stimuli that have made you lose your mind in the past, step back, pause, inhale, and remember strategic silence.

When you are turning red and about to lose it, strategic silence is your only friend. My only friend is strategic taciturnity. Repeat that to yourself. Then, shut up!

Take care to shut up. Assess the jam you are in for what it is, which is nine times out of ten another human being trying to have their way with you in a power grab situation of one type or another. Just shut up. That is quite often the only de-escalation technique ever needed.

Serve or disengage. Then, release the person or group. Offer forgiveness to the other as well as to thyself for entering such emotionally testy entanglements in the first place. Forgiveness is your shield. Forgiveness removes any attachment you have to the situation and has a cleansing benefit that should be applied to all involved.

Give it a shot. When you fall. Get back up. Try it again. Until you get it. This is the most important exercise in many respects because getting a hold on your out of control infantile reactive self can be the difference between making millions of dollars and being flat broke. The difference between robust health and abject infirmity. The difference between living happy and free and being shackled to a large barrel of stinky negativity. It is up to you. Choose your own adventure.

Be aware that your choices have real consequences that will ensue following your course of action. If you choose to covet your neighbor's partner, wealth, talent, or other gifts and attributes, you will fail to find peace. Stop looking externally for validation. Stop looking for material satisfaction.

Get to work on yourself. Covet Self-Realization.

Lesson Six

Covet Self-Realization

Another trademark of the divinely masculine boy or man is that he is a relentless connoisseur of what Paramahansa Yogananda referred to as self-realization. Yogananda was a gifted prophet and spiritual teacher who traversed the Atlantic Ocean by steamship to teach spiritual awakening in America in the 1920s. Yogananda's life was remarkable from cradle to grave.

I encourage each of you to research Paramahansa Yogananda. There is a great documentary on his life entitled "Awake: The Life of Yogananda." Check it out tonight in lieu of wasting your time on video games or crap reality television.

Many teachers have come to the earth to guide humanity on the path of spiritual evolutionary awakening. Yogananda was one such teacher. He taught us that power over others, and over things, is ephemeral, giving rise to suffering through attachment. Like fool's gold, in the hands of an amateur speculator, seeking ephemeral external power is an illusion. Stop looking for the Holy Grail. You are the Holy Grail! Go inward. Go deep.

Power over thyself is the only true power. It is power over thyself that serves to reduce suffering through external attachment reduction. If you want a real, lasting, blissful being in this lifetime, aim inward. Covet self-understanding and self-reliance.

Self-realization is the way of the divinely masculine boy or man. Take the helm of your own mind and govern your words and actions according to your principles of living that you have set forth for yourself. We have all been told that covetousness is a sin, a deadly sin. Yet, if we are to be covetous should we not covet spiritual emancipation for ourselves? For the other 7.7 billion suffering human beings walking the earth today?

Covetousness is indeed sinful in the majority of cases. No doubt. That is one hundred percent definitely the case when someone covets crack cocaine, violence against themselves or others, etc. Do not covet things that are harmful to you or are harmful to others. Unshackle yourself from the temptations in your life.

Insulate yourself from the normal cacophony of covetousness that people have come to see as normal within our current consumption based reality. The need to own things, which end up owning us in the end, is primarily driven by fear masqueraded as egotistical narcissism. Stop playing the game.

The very nature of the human being innately seems to lend itself to such extremes without self-awareness and proper self-governance. If we must be covetous, we should covet self-realization exclusively. Yogananda envisaged self-realization as the permeation of a knowing, infusing the body, mind, and soul, that we are all one with the omnipresence of God. Yogananda was the real deal. A bona fide enlightened individual. We, as a society, still have much to learn from him.

Self-realization is the ultimate endgame for all human beings, whether we know it now or not. Indeed, achieving self-realization is rare. But walking that path to self-realization has many pleasant surprises, windfalls, and unexpected fortuitous occurrences within itself. What is holding you back?

You might fall back on old narratives about how unfair and abusive your parents were to you. How your public school system failed you. Why you couldn't get into the college of your choice because of your income or race. Why you were passed over for the promotion at work again. On and on you will go.

Stop blaming your circumstances or your lack of innate abilities for limiting your life experiences.

Those are all excuses and serve but one purpose. They keep the vibration of suffering alive in your human bodily vessel. Try to unchain yourself from them. Dwelling on the past does nothing for your future. You must learn from it and move on.

The primary hindrance to embarking down the road of self-realization is the desire for human beings to conform to mainstream thoughts and actions. Like the great teacher Earl Nightingale told us: the problem today is not cowardice. The problem is conformity.

Everyone is trying so hard to be just like everyone else while simultaneously trying to appear more woke than the next person.

No matter what we do, the collectivist mentality ultimately ends up collapsing in on itself.

Stand for individualism. Stand for freedom. Respect others' opinions, but stand up for what is right.

There is no real civil discourse left in America today. All too often now when people disagree with us, the ad hominem attacks start and continue ad nauseum.

The issue is that things end up boiling down to a binary when it comes to identity. It is either black or white, and nobody wants to acknowledge that grey exists. People become so rooted in what they identify as that they don't even bother trying to listen to what those on the other side of the fence are trying to say. What happened to being open-minded?

All too often, hate speech has supplanted healthy, serious, and informative discussion. Actual critical thinking be damned!

This is all useless and boring and doesn't move anyone forward.

Can you believe that? Look around for yourself. Conduct your own analysis. People are walking around all day staring down at their phones, parroting the thoughts and actions of others. The funny thing is that they are so sucked into this way of being they don't even register that they have fallen victim to groupthink.

Have the courage to separate yourself from the autonomous herd before they bring you down or destroy your life completely.

One person's externally directed happiness has been incentivized to become a zero-sum game against another's version of externally directed happiness. Most people are playing a very shallow game of life wherein even the supposed winners in life lose big. Just look how happy, and well-balanced, our favorite masculine celebrities are. What a farce!

Very few of us think of ourselves as free, rational, and self-interested individuals who should be judged by the content of our characters rather than the color of our skin, what political party we voted for, or where we worship a god of our understanding.

Nope. Nowadays it is all about skin color, background, microaggressions both seen and unseen, and a whole bunch of other alphabet soup gobbledygook crap that no one seems to really understand.

There is so much nastiness and divisiveness afoot. It is altogether not serving our highest interests, individually nor collectively. Do not define yourself by the other. Avoid the trap of sorrow at another's good. Stand for the individual freedom of every other American citizen, the First Amendment rights of each and every American citizen, and the right of all American citizens to live free from violence. Before we set out to save the world, let us heal the United States of America.

Respect yourself. Respect others. Do not fall into the trap of sorrow at another's good.

Avoiding the Trap of Sorrow at Another's Good

Florence Welch, the entertaining and talented lead singer in the indie rock band Florence and the Machine, is an avowed feminist. I found that out later after doing a bit of post-show research. The bass and drums were rhythmic and driving. Really rocking hard. The barefoot Welch sang energetically while doing pirouettes in a long, flowing banshee dress. It was all very entertaining.

Somewhere on a break between songs, Florence Welch began to address the issues of the day, speaking extemporaneously to a mesmerized crowd who hung on her every word.

Welch said verbatim that there probably is "not much toxic masculinity at a Florence and the Machine Show" (Florence Welch, 2019). I thought to myself, probably not.

In fact, I had not seen any examples of toxic masculinity that entire day as I had been too busy enjoying the concert experience. However, as a man who had purchased a ticket, it felt like a discriminatory slap in my face. No matter what we always have to be reminded of our differences. The illusion of togetherness rears its ugly head again!

From the time I queued up in line for the show, I interacted with both men and women. Adults and children. Everyone there was actually quite helpful. We all were happy to be in congenial attendance to hear the show. Despite any evidence of toxic masculinity, it still had to be brought up!

There always must be some. Some toxic masculinity is always going to be in any social environment due to the residue of the institutional biases that pervade the very structure of the society in which we live. I get many believe that. It is astounding how prevalent groupthink has become in the age of high technology and low spiritual understanding.

It occurred to me that, no matter the circumstances, there could never be absolutely no toxic masculinity in a public entertainment venue.

The time is upon us wherein we must seriously ask ourselves if we have taken all of the histrionics, and the choreographed sound bite outrage, just a bit too far. At the concert that night, I saw human beings, with many men and boys in the audience, interacting peaceably and enjoying the sweet sounds of Florence's harmonies.

Overall, I really enjoyed the show. Florence had a rock-solid rhythm section. I would advise my readers who have never heard of Florence and the Machine to check them out when they come to your town. It is an awesome performance surrounded by very cool Florence fans.

Know that the majority of people that you encounter in this world will not be of the enlightened variety, even if they have other performance talents. Be patient with all. Including yourself.

Your average human being has been steeped these days, since prekindergarten, in victim-based thinking grounded in identity politics. Forgive them. Serve or disengage. Limit your exposure going forward.

Much of identity politics is about power. You do not have to internalize the lies of identity politics to get power for yourself. Guard against doing so. That type of internalization will only serve to stultify your intellectual, physical, and spiritual growth. Much more power is to be realized when you cultivate your inner gifts and begin to manifest the reality you seek through walking the path of self-refinement and self-realization.

The truest act of rebellion, in this pathetic cesspool culture, is the outright rejection of identity politics altogether.

Beware, even if you are on the very path of righteousness, most people will have preconceived notions of your toxicity before you open your mouth or interact with them in any way just because of your plumbing. Where is the outrage over that fact? There will be none. It must begin with the boys and men ourselves. We must stand up for ourselves and heal one another at this time, my friends.

It is time that we all come to an agreement on a new set of rules. To govern ourselves. To govern our communities. To govern our states. To govern our nation. This new set of rules must be predicated upon respect for thyself and respect for others.

Respect thyself and all others at all times. In all situations. No matter what. Follow that path.

Embody divinely masculine traits with the highest levels of earnestness and sincerity, and you will come into an existence that is well beyond any life that you could have previously imagined. Become a free thinking, liberated, highly-conscious individual in this lifetime. Do not internalize the low vibrational frequencies of identity politics. Identity politics is a dead-end road.

Reject Identity Politics!

Identity politics focuses on the gender, skin color, and sexual proclivity of a human being ahead of the content of one's character. Individual accountability and achievement be damned. This is the age of toxic Orwellian tribalism, don't you know?

As the great Dr. Martin Luther King, Jr. taught, it should be about the content of one's character not the color of one's skin, but it is not. In fact, today's divisive identity politics reverses the teachings of Dr. King. On purpose. For power. It is insidious. It must be stopped.

Instead of focusing on teaching boys and men to take individual accountability for their own life deliverables in pursuance of arete, generations of both boys and men have been inculcated with victim-based groupthink assumptions regarding gender, race, and sexual proclivity that just quite simply run contrary to the reality of the actual lived human experience. Victimization think, and victimization speak, lead invariably, and quite inevitably, to victimization behaviors against thyself and the greater society at large.

Identity politics is transforming our country into a toxic, tribalistic Orwellian nightmare. Wherein everyone must guard against offending everyone else, all the time.

These days, no matter what you say or do, there will be immense criticism lodged your way. Incoming! Often by those who disagree with you politically. There is no civility left in this toxically tribalistic society, my friends.

As a divinely masculine man walking your path, take great care to avoid controversy. Do not walk into such traps. The pitfalls you will be ambushed with, due to your plumbing alone, will be enough to deal with.

Remember, these days you do not even have to do anything wrong to be hogtied and slapped down by the henchmen, and women, of the media.

Identify with your individuality, expressed and demonstrated through your values and virtues. Memorialized through your high achievements in this lifetime. Do not go through life leading with gender identification, racial identification, or sexual proclivity identification. It matters not whether you identify as male or female. Whatever socially constructed race you believe yourself to be at this time, or whether in terms of sexual proclivity, you are straight, gay, bi, trans, or somewhere else in the alphabet soup of sexual orientation identification these days. Let all of that go. It is getting really boring.

You are not any of those categories. We are all individuals. Children of God. Begin to wake up to both your own divinity as well as the divinity in others. None of those aforementioned categories matter whatsoever.

What does matter is how you treat yourself and, subsequently, how you treat others. What does matter is what you accomplish on the earth in this lifetime. Personal empowerment is enlivening. Identity politics is enfeebling.

We are not our sex. We are not our gender. We are not our race. We are not our color. We are not our sexual proclivity. We are all in need of love and understanding. We are all humans. We are all children of God.

This is all a part of the illusion of separateness, my friends.

Consider this.

Those of us human bodily vessels born biologically male, still have a feminine side of our bodies and brains. Likewise, those born biologically female, still have a masculine side of their bodies and brains.

It is the very acme of foolishness for one to constantly throw hate-filled barbs at the target of what they are erroneously envisaging as the opposite sex. Such vicious people obviously have little self-understanding.

People who are man or woman-haters are usually disconnected from their true natures. Predominantly, they are self-haters who project venom onto the erroneously perceived opposite. Their idea of a villain.

It is at the heart of the very illusion of separateness.

Wake up from the illusion of separateness. See through it.

We all have a Shiva side. We all have a Shakti side. Balanced and enlightened human beings have come to terms with both their masculine and feminine sides. Become free from the illusion of separateness. The illusion of separateness is the chief force catalyzing so much unnecessary pain and suffering.

The illusion of separateness leads people down the rabbit hole of actually buying into the notion that the opposite sex is their arch nemesis.

Release the idea that all women are a certain way. Release the idea that all men are a certain way. Let that all go. Begin today to treat people as individuals, giving them the benefit of the doubt all while conducting yourself professionally at all times. With absolutely no exceptions. None whatsoever.

Treat people with respect by first respecting yourself. Also, do not take offense when someone obliviously prejudges you as a masculine Darth Vader figure solely based on the illusion of separateness.

Do not retaliate. If you do not accept the given insult or slight, it will be returned to the sender. Outside of school or work, serve or disengage in those situations and walk away. At school or work take care to document the mistreatment for administration and human resources just in case they need to become involved as a remedy for such abuse.

Outside of work or school, terminate toxic relationships in your life with a resounding sense of finality. Closure is grounded in permanence. Do not get bogged down in a new toxically tribalistic Orwellian world that despises the divinely masculine.

You are not a man. She is not a woman. That is an illusion. You are both. You are none. The one that is two. The two that is one. Escape the illusion of separateness. Danger, Will Robinson.

We are all children of God. Some born representative of the masculine vibration. Shiva. Some born representative of the feminine vibration. Shakti. It is axiomatic. There is no debate. One simply cannot exist without the other.

Throughout the majority of human history, and still occurring within some circles today, the illusion of separateness has been omnipresent to create racial disparities, catalyzing disputes and worse.

Throughout the entirety of our nation's history, black Americans have been treated terribly by racists and through public policy. It took hundreds of years for federal and state laws to change. But there is still so much work to do.

Racial bigotry should simply not be tolerated in our academic, business, and outwardly societal dealings with one another.

Race is a very emotional issue for people given treatment of minorities. Yet, the public policy has changed in that area. People are slow to catch up, apparently.

Race provides another glimpse into the inherently divisive nature at the very core of the illusion of separateness.

Really if you think about it, all human beings are really of one race: the human race.

That should be the starting point for our discussions on race going forward. Race is important today for all unimportant reasons, typically grounded in arguments derived from divisive identity politics. We need to come to a much more nuanced understanding of race and the social condition. Race is a social construction that has been used to divide and conquer the human population for eons. Until enough people wake up to this notion, this unfortunate trend will most certainly continue.

Consider this. In the mid-twentieth century, there were signs all over New York City saying, "Irish and Colored Need Not Apply." Those businesses did not hire the Irish because they were not considered "white" at the time. Same with the Italians, who are often referred to as "white" today, as they were not considered to be "white" at the time. Do not let stereotypical ideas define you or shape, guide, or steer your course of thought or action in any way, shape, or form.

What is white? What is black? What is tan? For me, in particular, what is peach? None of that matters. Treat the other as an individual worthy of love, respect, honor, and prestige. The very same you would want for yourself. Take that approach continuously. Without fail, you will be surprised with the results that come your way. Danger, Will Robinson

Thirdly, just as we are not our gender and we are not our race, we are also not our sexual proclivity.

For centuries, homosexuals have been treated poorly in the West. Their basic civil liberties and human rights were trampled upon. It was shameful. Yet, today we have taken the remedies for such poor treatment in the past too far. Way too far!

There are too many alphabet soup acronyms, and other gobbledygook nonsense to remember, because you still end up offending people, nonetheless. For boys and men there is only one way to safely operate in this toxic society that we find ourselves in today. Keep your professional life professional. Keep your private life private. Hint, your sexual proclivity should be housed in the private life, not professional life, category. Just for those who did not know.

Who cares with whom you are sharing intimacy? As long as it is a consensual relationship, why does it matter?

Also, I will say this once. Do not prey on minors.

Conduct yourself accordingly.

Your sexual proclivity is your private business. It is not to be advertised on social media. Respect yourself. Respect others. Most importantly, for those of you in relationships, show immense respect to your partners.

Respect given leads to respect earned. With the always omnipresent assumption that toxic relationships should be immediately terminated, move forth on that path today.

Sexual proclivity is nothing to be celebrated. It is a minor part of a complex human life. What should be celebrated instead would be the individual accomplishments and the content of the character of the individual in question. Danger, Will Robinson.

Now that we have covered what we are not, let's get to what are we. This is the part of the story that I love the most.

This is what we are!

We are our ideas, our words, our behaviors, actions, and deeds, and we are spiritual beings. Begin to focus on the refinement of your thinking and your words, and your behaviors, actions, and deeds will soon follow. It all starts with your thinking.

We are our ideas.

Your life is the penultimate manifestation of the flow of your thoughts. For you to begin walking the path of strategic self-reinvention, you must first take the helm of your own mind. Begin to recognize your errant thoughts. The negative limiting ones such as, "I am not good enough," that have been holding you back from fulfilling your life purpose and truly experiencing raw bliss in this lifetime. Replace those negative thoughts with this positive mantra: "health, wealth, and happiness."

When a detectable errant thought comes up in your stream of consciousness, correct it by saying that mantra twelve times to clear the errant notion from your energetic human bodily vessel. It is helpful to place the thumb and index finger together saying the mantra three times. Then the thumb, index finger, and middle finger together saying the mantra three times. Adding the ring finger to the bunch next saying the mantra three times. Concluding with the positioning of the little finger with the entirety of the bunch, saying the mantra three times. That is a trick to ensure that the twelve-time mantra recitation clearing power is turned up to maximum wattage.

We are our words.

Just as we must watch what we put in our mouths, we too must govern what comes out of our mouths.

Nowadays, people have the incessant need, seemingly reaching obsessional proportions, to express themselves. Posting on social media continuously about the trivial peculiarities of the lives of ultra-rich celebrities, all of which have sold their souls a long time ago. Living entirely disconnected from the reality of their adoring fans.

When these worshipers of the inane are not posting to social media, they are expressing themselves by text. Usually with acronyms that do not have one-tenth of the explanatory power needed to communicate the complexities of human life existence. The dumbing down of life led by softies afflicted by a certain readily identifiable dependency, TES.

Talk less. Listen more. Study yourself and the world around you. Say what you mean. Mean what you say. Never allow the peer pressure of the groupthink mob to pressure you to do harm to yourself or others. Your health, your wealth, and your happiness are valuable commodities. Protect them.

Do not be the boy or man who yells at others in traffic. They have been getting shot lately. Do not be the type of boy or man who verbally abuses people who are weaker. Remember that your words have power. A cutting power. Words are instruments. Instruments can be used for God's grace, or they can be weaponized. Words have power to maim and destroy. Words have power to save and heal. Choose how you use them.

We are our behaviors, actions, and deeds.

The cumulation of our thinking and words adds up to our behaviors, actions, and deeds. This is serious business, gentlemen. Wake up. Errant thinking, and running your big mouth, can get you killed. Literally.

Contrarily, responsible thinking about personal accountably, and making use of strategic taciturnity, can launch you on the path of unimaginable success and prosperity.

The choice is up to you. The time is your own to use toward the advancement of your spiritual evolution, or the time is your own to use toward the furtherance of life misery and suffering as well. Either way, with or without your knowledge, understanding, or approval, this is a spiritual life, and you are having spiritual experiences in this lifetime either consciously, or less so.

We are spiritual beings undergoing refinement. Wake up to this reality and begin treating yourself, as well as all of those around you, as such. What do you really have to lose? The dead-end path you are currently on will continue administering severe beatings on the daily until morale improves, or you could walk a different path. An inward path. A path of individual self-realization, cultivating arete in all areas of your life existence.

Go Inward & Covet Self-Realization, Cultivating Arete in All Areas of Your Life

Ubiquitously, human beings seek external validation. When you were a small child, it was absolutely necessary to your survival for you to go outward. You could not provide for yourself. So, commencing at day one of most human life existences, the outward seeking programming begins. You see it in your everyday walk through life. Advertisements for the experts abound.

You need a lawyer for this. Well, if you had made better decisions, you probably would not have needed that expert attorney.

You need a doctor for this. Well if you had eaten sunlight foods, practiced yoga, and meditated daily, you could have probably avoided that health scare.

You need to get advice on taking a home equity loan from your financial expert. Well, if you had budgeted better, stopped people pleasing and set healthier financial boundaries with your transactions, and tithed to thyself as a hard and fast solid rule each month a mere ten percent of every dollar you earned, you would not have ever been in that financial predicament in the first place.

As you may have already realized from your reading of this text, and the exercises herein that you have been practicing, we all volunteer for the majority of the life problems that beset our individual, and collective, experiences. We needed the expert mommy and daddy once upon a time as helpless young tikes. Yet, once you reach that fend-for-yourself age, it becomes gravely important – for your own intellectual, emotional, and spiritual evolution – for you to develop an equal or greater capacity for going inward.

Continuously looking to the expert, as an adult, is a sure sign that you must go back to the drawing board to reevaluate the manner in which you are thinking, eating, and what programming you are subjecting yourself to and why. Then, you must draw correlations between the aforementioned and the words and utterances that you put forth and the actions, behaviors, and deeds that you carry out.

In all of your words and actions focus on arete.

If external seeking is the cause of much of suffering, how do we go inward? First and foremost, as we have already discussed previously in this book get rid of your social media, video games, and other distractions. Make use of strategic silence. Read this book daily. Practice the exercises herein daily. Make time for meditation daily.

Put your health, wealth, and happiness first as you create your definite life purpose in the overall context of your life mission, carry out that life purpose, and serve others. Stop focusing on external validation, on external expert advice – which is usually contravened by another expert opinion in short order – and begin cultivating your own intuitive inner knowing.

Most people get stretched way too thin hustling to go from here or there, doing what must be done to get through school or work. Many people waste incredible amounts of time wasting away on the social media, playing video games, and watching the idiot box.

Then, on top of it all, many people have myriad little hobbies, none of which they are particularly good at doing. Karaoke and golf come to mind. Few that actually generate any revenue coming in for them. All serve to whittle away the remainder of any time that would have been left for definite life purpose self-creation and pursuance work.

Mediocrity is the general rule. Often, people fall short of that mark. Yet, that does not have to be your life existence. You can reinvent yourself personally and evolve into the person that you really want to be. As you continue to eliminate your distractions and work the exercises in this book, you will both create your definite life purpose and learn to love the pursuit of such to the very ends of the earth if need be.

The love of the definite life purpose work that you have chosen is grounded in the notion of the pursuance of arete. Arete can only be achieved through a daily, almost ritualistic, pounding on your craft. Continuously accessing better training, new information, and gaining motivation to be the very best in the world at your particular definite life purpose creation.

The pursuit of arete through such brings joyous satisfaction to what would have otherwise been a mundane human existence. You will know you are on the path of the pursuance of arete in your viscera.

Learn to trust your gut. Your viscera is your gut. You have heard people state that they have a good gut feeling about someone or something. To have a visceral feeling is tantamount to saying that the notion was intuitive. Intuition and the viscera go hand and hand. The prescience to develop a visceral understanding of both life and the living of it can indeed confer tremendous social, business, and even dating advantages upon the holder of the keys of such understanding. Tipping one off to what may lie ahead can do that for a person.

Keeping the tiny fire of inner seeking alive until it burgeons into a wildfire, a veritable alchemically transformable conflagration. That is exactly what Michael Jordan did.

The Michael Jordan Story

"I've missed more than 9,000 shots in my career. I've lost almost 300 games. Twenty-six times, I've been trusted to take the game-winning shot and missed. I've failed over and over and over again in my life. And that is why I succeed" (Michael Jordan).

The stories far and wide, regarding Michael Jordan's indefatigable work ethic, are legendary. He never took any aspect of his game for granted.

Jordan was the king of the game day preparation. Frontloading his physical, mental, and spiritual training so he could be ever ready and continuously present on gameday. Jordan's mantra was back to the fundamentals constantly.

If you have the fundamentals down, your foundation will be solid. If you train hard with that solid foundation in place your game can become unstoppable. Indeed, Jordan's did. Drilling the fundamentals is key in both sports and in life. Drilling the fundamentals is essential to the achievement of greatness.

Greatness does not manifest by happenstance. Greatness is the coagulative consequence of the convergence of many variables. Right thinking comes first. Jordan wanted to win. He wanted to win badly. Jordan knew that he had to first sow before he could reap the victory that was his already in his own mind's eye. He just had to show the rest of us. He did just that.

Jordan sowed by relentlessly practicing and drilling the fundamentals. He reaped on the scoreboard. Jordan was a master of forgetting his failures while maintaining a steady presence in the present moment wherein he expected his shots to go in. Go in they did. He expected to win because he had prepared better than the opponents. Yet, even while in the light of his great accomplishments, Jordan always maintained civility and decorum in his public life. Demonstrating humility and class in complete success and victory is Jordan's signature drink. Try a sip.

You do not see Michael Jordan's twitter account controversies being mentioned in the news. That is because there are none. Jordan makes great use of strategic silence. Moreover, his digital footprint is squeaky clean.

Learn from Jordan. Drill the fundamentals constantly. Your greatest accomplishments can only come to fruition if you have set yourself ready to play on a solid foundation. In greatness, learn from Jordan, demonstrate humility. If you have the fundamentals of your craft down, you will have a solid foundation for life success.

What comes immediately to mind when you think of your foundation? Hint, you are indeed what you eat. Remember GIGO? The very first foundation that should come to mind is the nutritional fundamentals and the nutritional foundation that you are providing for your human bodily vessel.

As mentioned throughout the book, your eating plan is your very foundation in this life existence. So, with Lesson Six, just as we have done in the previous lessons, it is now time to switch the gears in preparation for the You Are What You Eat Exercise Six. This lesson, my friends, we will focus upon the concept of eating the rainbow of light.

You Are What You Eat Exercise 6: Eat the Rainbow of Sunlight Foods

The sixth You Are What You Eat exercise focuses on eating the rainbow. As you may have noticed in your meditational exercises, there is a color associated with each of the lesson's meditations.

Those colors are associated with the various energetic centers that comprise the human bodily system. Many different traditions have shown light around spiritually advancing individuals. The halo around Jesus Christ and some Saints is a primary Judeo-Christian example. The Tibetan rainbow body is another such example. In the East, the chakras also portray the human bodily vessel as an ascending sequence of rainbow light.

It would only make sense if we seek to enhance the functioning of those energetic centers, within our own human bodily vessels, that we would eat sunlight foods from all areas of the color spectrum.

I know. This all sounds outrageously foreign to you in this day and age where scientists have it all down. It is about calorie counting, carb loading, fad dieting, or whatever the rage is today in the multi-billion-dollar weight loss industry.

From an outside perspective, it looks like the purpose of the weight loss industry is not at all to help people lose weight, but to create customers reliant upon whatever snake oil concoction they are peddling at the moment.

The truth is quite simple: eat a primarily plant-based meal plan, exercise physically, and meditate daily so you will never need to throw your money away again.

If the scientists, and the supposedly all-knowing weight loss industry really had it all down, why on earth are we at a point where over 75% of men and boys in the West are either suffering with various levels of obesity and overweightness?

Let go of your need for an expert. Eat primarily plant-based and eat the rainbow. You will be utterly astounded by the results.

Workout Exercise 6: Swimming

Workout Exercise Six focuses on swimming. Swimming is a great full-body, low-impact workout that will really take your cardiovascular health and well-being to the next level if you pursue your swimming goals with high intensity regular training.

In an Olympic sized pool, thirty-three laps is the distance of a one-mile swim. So that is your goal. To jump into the pool and to swim steadily with a consistent pace in command of your breath up and back thirty-three times.

I like to start out lap one with the freestyle stroke, and I come back on the even laps doing the breaststroke. I push hard on my odd laps, freestyling my way down the pool lane and seeing the black line through my foggy frog-man goggles. Then, I relax, regroup, and reobtain my breath on the even breaststroke laps in preparation for the upcoming freestyling frenzy.

I personally like to swim with a diver's mask and snorkel. The high-quality mask and snorkel set allow for unimpeded air flow that fuels your mile-long swim.

Others may prefer to wear goggles only and to turn their heads to the side for air during freestyle. Try both. They both have training value.

Start where you are, especially if you are new to the practice of swimming. What I mean by start where you are is not to get down on yourself if you cannot swim thirty-three laps in a row with continuous breath control on your first day out.

Set goals and work up to the achievement of those goals. If you have any question about what a solid swimming exercise practice will bring to your life, just see how ripped Olympic swimmers are on the medal platforms. We might be able to learn a little something from those swimmers.

Meditation Exercise 6: Indigo

Begin Meditation Exercise Six with the lung stretching deep pranayama breathing warm up technique. Now, bring your attention to your eyebrow center which is indigo in color. This energy center vibrates with the A note Om. This energy is associated with the deadly sin of envy and the golden virtue of liberality.

You may have heard of the pineal gland in your readings and musings on esoteric topics. The pineal gland has fascinated mankind since the early days of humanity. The ancient Sumerian writings make mention of this divine glandular organ located just between your eyebrows. The Seat of the Soul is how the great philosopher Rene Descartes referred to the pineal gland. Like you did with the other energy centers see the golf ball size indigo energy of intuition swirling at your forehead center.

Bring the audible, or inaudible, vibrational intonation of the A note Om to life inflating the golf ball to the size of an orange, then to the size of a basketball. Consciously paste your tongue to the roof of your mouth. Continue with that vibrational intonation. Now, retract your tongue from the roof of your mouth. Feel the difference.

Understand that your tongue, pasted to the roof of your mouth, creates a divine circuit that allows the energies racing up the spinal highway to cross the tongue bridge. Emanating fully into the roof of the mouth, shooting directly upward into the frontal lobe and forehead.

Practice tongue up and tongue down three times. Then, double down on your A note vibrational intonation Om pulling your belly button into the spine enlarging the indigo sphere to encompass and completely consume your entire bodily vessel. Feel the A note pulsing the energy within your forehead center. This enlivening, activation, and subsequent awakening will confer an enhanced set of intuitive skills to your life. Skills that enhance your health, wealth, and happiness and create a satisfaction with life, infused with very high and extraordinarily rare levels of self-reliance, self-healing, and overall well-being and wellness.

Feel a tapping on your forehead center as you audibly pulse that A note. When you feel complete, bring the indigo sphere down to the size of a basketball. Then, bring it down to the size of the orange. Finally, return to a balanced state of harmony. Bring it down in size to the golf ball. Envy will not limit your life experiences today.

The Cultivation of Arete in All Areas of Your Life Exercise

This is the sixth of seven exercises that will allow you to apply what you have learned, in each of the seven lessons in this book, in real-world decision-making application. We already know arete denotes excellence.

Connotatively, arete speaks to one's moral virtue. One's moral virtue as it relates to the fulfillment of one's highest purpose or potential.

You see arete in action when people have devised a definite life purpose and are sharpening themselves for the task.

Arete on the Saturday gridiron field when the Hail Mary pass is caught in the endzone to win the game just before time elapses. They drilled that by the way!

You see it on the concert stage in the concertmaster, or lead violinist for you non-musician people. Arete abounds in various small businesses all around your community. Arete exists wherever human beings have created positive definite life purpose in the overall context of their life missions, wherein they are actively in pursuance of such.

Identifying arete for what it really is is actually quite simple. It is the unbounded capacity of the wonder of the human consciousness. It is the power of love, internal love for us, that consciously radiates outward to the world. Through the justly benevolent treatment of others.

There is no better enjoyment in life than the creation of your definite life purpose in the context of your overall life mission and the pursuance of such. True fulfillment, based in sowing and reaping thereafter, is the most liberating experience we human beings can undertake. Stop being a spectator in the game of life. Decide right now exactly what it is that you really want to do and achieve in this lifetime.

Get to definiteness of purpose first. What is it that you truly want to achieve in this lifetime? Develop a PSLP to guide the way. Set measurable goals. Work like hell to bring your vision to fruition. Enjoy the journey, the hardships, the plateaus, peaks, and valleys. Traverse the spiritual path emboldened by your steadfast commitment to bringing your vision into this reality.

Really, the cultivation of arete in all areas of your life exercise is an exercise in reductive elimination. Eliminate the distractions that are keeping you from the creation of your definite life purpose.

As said distractions fall away, you will become much more present in your school or work environments. Begin where you are. Be the best student, or the best worker, that you can possibly be.

In class, move to the front. Ask questions. Participate. Do the homework. Know it. Aim for the 'A+'.

At work, double down on patience. Listen to your supervisor and do your best to make their life easier because they have you on board. Be professional with everyone at all times in the workplace. No exceptions whatsoever. Guard your professional reputation with your life.

You will find that when you begin to cultivate arete where you are currently, things get a whole lot simpler. Stop fighting everything, or everybody, all the time.

Flow through your day like water, totally unaffected by the stressors poking you from the left and jabbing you from the right.

Breathe. Focus on being present.

Do a great job with everyone you come in contact with that day. Then, get off work or out of school and revisit your PSLP so you can begin the work that will unveil the next, more improved, chapter of your victorious story. The one that will be retold for generations.

Lesson Seven

Strength Needs No Introduction

The divinely masculine strive to live their lives in a conscious state of humble teachability. Being humbly teachable is the path to empowerment. The ego-driven, fear-based notion that you know it already is really grounded in problems of affluence.

People are very entitled and indolent these days. Many do not want to put in the work. Awakening spiritually and pursuing the inner work that allows for life, liberty, and the pursuit of happiness is arduous. Those who walk the path of self-realization will realize the reward. We reap what we sow. The key to understanding that passage is to know that the sowing comes first!

You will notice that when you really stop for a minute and take a look around, the people who are placing all of their eggs in the baskets of materialism, CRAP Frankenfood, smart device addiction, and political conflict are unquestionably some of the most miserable sons of guns you will ever encounter on this planet. These are the people that simply do not know that they do not know. Danger, Will Robinson!

Do not fall into the pernicious trap of not knowing what you do not know. It is insidious and highly contagious as birds of a collectivist feather flock together. Avoid groups of people who do not have their own, or your own, best interests in mind front and center. Avoid falling prey to groupthink.

Remember the wise words of Bruce Lee about the emptying of the teacup.

The old tea must be discarded to make room for new tea.

Moral of the story?

Remain teachable. Remain humble.

Learn all you can from all those paths you cross. Do the work. Let the ego crap go. It is holding you back. The divinely masculine person steadily progresses toward arete in all areas of life.

Superman does not need to announce to people that he has arrived at a fight. They know.

Likewise, when you are the best at your game, others will take notice. They will go on and on about how talented and successful you are, and they will wonder how you got there. You know the truth.

You are on top because you developed a definite life purpose, trained like hell to refine your skill set, and pursued arete to the ends of the earth. No one sees the hard work, training, blood, sweat, tears, and sleepless nights.

There is no need to tell them all about it. Just nod, smile, and acknowledge the individual who gave you a compliment. Do not expect people to kiss the ring either. Hard and fast rule here.

When it comes to criticism, never react with anger or a hostile reply. Instead, open your ears and learn as much as you can. Often, the harshest critics are the ones who will help you succeed the most. They will push you to do and be better.

The best and only way to reply to criticism is to let your actions speak for themselves. Shut your mouth. Do not make any social media posts about it. Do not send the critic a snarky text. Suppress the urge to react. Slap that strategic silence card down, walk away, and begin working on the refinement of your game.

A professional athlete recently threatened a journalist who had been critical of his performance for quite some time over social media. As a consequence, he was released from his contract and kicked off the team. Was that the best way of handling that situation on his part?

Fine, maybe the journalist was being cantankerous, but we can't just threaten all of our critics.

We would end up with stacks of lawsuits and warrants for criminal prosecution. Hard and fast rule here, guys.

Never threaten anyone.

It is always, always, always wrong to do so. At any time. For any reason.

Could things have ended differently for that professional athlete?

The answer is yes. Yes, things could have. The athlete could have chosen to put his device down and regroup, vowing to be better prepared, and healed up for the next game. If the professional athlete had come back strongly in that next game, the journalist would have had to eat his words.

Instead of affording himself the chance at redemption, that professional athlete gave into the temptation to make those less than useful and totally inappropriate posts on the social media.

Take note: when you are making millions of dollars to play a child's game, thank your lucky stars. Certainly, never throw away your winning ticket just because your insecurities can't handle what some punk critic has to say about you. The best revenge is improved behavior, speech, and thought.

Do you really think that journalist would have wanted to go hand-to-hand with that professional athlete? No way.

The professional athlete lost his cool, subsequently throwing away what could have been a very good career path with his team.

It is okay to expect respect, just be prepared to give it to everyone you come across too. Treat others with respect so they will respect you. Even if you perceive them to be disrespectful to you, respect them. Kill them with kindness.

Either serve or disengage. Those people are quite literally not worth your time or anyone else's for that matter. Do not allocate any of your invaluable energy towards worrying over those types of folks.

From this day forward, stop wasting your time on the ideas, words, actions, and the affairs of others. Focus on your own health, wealth, and happiness, and know it will be achieved through collaboration, cooperation, and communication with like-minded others who are pursuing the same things as you.

Living masterfully creates strange bedfellows. Just as strength needs no introduction, neither does peace. We know both when we see them for sure.

If you want peace in your life, live strongly. Peace through strength is really your only best hope. Plan well. Act as if you know your shot is going to go in. Evaluate your performance. Keep drilling the fundamentals. Sharpen your skills. Cultivate your craft.

If you do those things with earnestness, and a sincere heart, you will win. In winning, new lessons will emerge.

The key is to beware the treacheries of the ego. The ego is a mighty convincing conman. See through the ego's gimmicks. Don't buy the snake oil. Instead, know that winning with humility is the path to take. Avoid the pride scale imbalance trap.

Avoiding the Pride Scale Imbalance Trap

The ego is a fascinating thing. It is needed to help preserve our lives in many ways, yet it is often tyrannical, out of control, and unwieldy. It waxes and wanes. Unless one has taken great pains to undertake the spiritual self-realization work to awaken in this lifetime, the ego convinces us of many things. Most of those things have kernels of truth, but they are planted in the wrong soil if you know what I mean. Pay close attention to the manner in which you evaluate your performance. Be sure to stay on the right side of the pride scale imbalance trap.

In the old days, before digital scales, the actual scale was important in the marketplace. Commerce depended on fair and accurate, agreed upon measurements so people could conduct business transactions properly, comparing apple to apple and orange to orange. Literally.

Back then, some merchants were known for having scales that were not fairly weighted. Those merchants quickly developed poor reputations.

Make sure that you – the one who will be doing your own self-evaluation – are using a fairly weighted scale when undertaking the measurement of someone's performance or activities. It is far easier to be the crooked merchant, with scales weighted to benefit the house, than it is to be honest with oneself.

But why would you not want to just get honest with where you are and where you want to be? Once that is known, bridging the gap becomes possible faster. You are worth it. Be honest in the way that you evaluate yourself. It will hurt. Be brutally honest when need be.

Brutal honesty – supplemented with a solid plan for life remediation, retooling, and retraining – is a far easier pill to swallow than the continuation of your current state of suffering. It is easier than knowing you will need a drink on the side to anesthetize yourself from the pain. Take life head on.

Be honest with yourself about how you are doing. Where is your Achilles heel?

Finding the balance between humility and confidence is predicated upon the notion that you are evaluating yourself using fairly weighted scales. Know your worth. Respect yourself through your respect for others. There is no need to harp on your life accomplishments. Some people simply love to hear themselves talk, their names called aloud; they love how others admire them, and they love when all attention is on them. Don't be this kind of person. Please. And if you are this person, right now, try to work on toning it down a bit. It probably rubs people the wrong way and it won't bring you happiness either.

The list of consequences that comes with hubris is too long to share. Just know that, historically, nothing has taken out more really talented, interesting, and successful people than hubris.

It is a silent killer. Do not let your ego write checks your body can not cash. Focus on your definite life purpose. Employ strategic silence. Make sure that your self-evaluation scales are fairly weighted. If evaluated upon fairly balanced scales and found to be wanting, do not react with overzealous, or threatening, words. Shut your big mouth. Put the device down. Get to work on fixing the problem. Demonstrate, do not explicate.

The Synergistic Nature of Humility and Arete

The good thing about success is that success quite often begets more success. This is especially true when the victor demonstrates authentic humility. Giving thanks to all the various people who came together to support your victory is legitimate if thanks are meant to be given. Mostly, the credit lies with you. You are the one who was up late and rose early. You are the one who stayed focused on the achievement of your definite life purpose. You deserve the credit. You got the victory.

There is no need to rub salt in the wounds of your opponents who are not as accomplished as you have come to be through your diligence, sacrifice, and tenacious pursuit of arete. No, it is far better to allow your performance, in whatever it is that you do, to stand for itself. Demonstrate, don't explicate.

The synergy of humility and arete igniting new realities is the name of this game. This is a real phenomenon. Just try it out. Be humble in your life's victories and watch as new opportunities come magically flooding into your life.

It may start as a slow trickle. Have faith. In time, if you keep your humble pursuit of arete up, you will be recognized for your efforts externally. The internal spiritual blessings, the ones that really matter, are already yours.

The synergy of humility and arete will take you far if you are able to develop the capacity to curtail your reactive tendencies. Make less emotional responses to triggering situations. In particular, never – no matter what transpires – allow another human being to bait you into some type of verbal or physical altercation.

Be prepared to defend yourself at all times; however, retreating whenever violent energies are foisted upon you is always your best bet.

If you are being attacked, retreat to a public place and call for help. Whether that is 911, your parents, or just a trusted friend would depend upon the severity of the situation at hand. To keep yourself out of trouble, here's a hard and fast rule for you.

Do not put your hands on anyone for any reason whatsoever (except of course in the case of justifiable self-defense). Even then, think twice, my friends.

No Fisticuffs! Never Lay Hands on Anyone Except in The Case of Highly Justifiable Self-Defense (Even then, think twice, my friends).

A charming, dapper, and rather long-haired young man came across my path back in my college days in my early twenties. He and I were dating two women who happened to be best friends. He was a good-looking, athletic young man who aspired to matriculate into the local law school after the completion of undergraduate school.

Upon getting to know this young man over the course of several months, I soon learned his story.

One day, about four years prior to meeting him, he had been out at a party drinking with friends. One of his mates had a big mouth. A real big one apparently. That friend ticked off a couple of the guys from a neighboring high school. A fight ensued.

The young man charged into the fight right behind his loud-mouthed buddy. He proceeded to unload fisticuffs on a few guys. One of the men was punched directly on the temple. He fell to the floor. That punch knocked him unconscious and he slipped into a coma later that evening.

He died in the intensive care unit (ICU) the next day.

The young man could have very well retreated from that melee. Instead, he chose to throw punches. One of those punches ended another person's life.

The young man was indicted, tried, and convicted by a judge on manslaughter charges. He served three years in prison.

In a setting that was not all too pleasant, that young man was able to regroup. After a lot of hard work on his part, he eventually went back to university.

Think before you act, gentlemen. Your aggression has consequences, and more often than not, you won't be able to predict what they are. Govern yourself accordingly.

Never threaten anyone. Never put your hands on anyone else. Unless you are legitimately in fear of losing your life.

Other than that, the hard and fast rule is very simple. Walk away. A lose-lose proposition fisticuffs has come to be. Is it really worth it?

I don't care how mad you are. I don't care what the other person called you, or what they said about your momma. Walk away.

I promise it will not make you look weak. In fact, it will make you look strong. Do you know how much strength someone has to have to walk away from a fight? From someone who is insulting them? People just want a reaction from you and if you give it to them, they win.

If you can retreat, you must retreat. There are not many situations out there where getting into a physical altercation will end up benefitting you in any way. It is the reactive fool that throws his career and future wealth down the toilet to physically prove a point to some idiot who probably has a lot less to lose.

Forgive them for being angry and for being an idiot. Give them a copy of this book! Pat them on the back and walk away. Move forward.

Obviously, not all altercations will let you walk away so easily, so to prepare for those off-chance moments (God forbid they don't happen to you), I recommend taking some type of martial arts classes and really hitting those weekly physical training exercises.

Without question, if you are attacked physically and you cannot retreat, I grant you permission to fight hard to defend yourself. That is your natural right. Fight hard and fight with honor. Fight to protect others.

If it comes to that, just be sure you can look back retrospectively - and you most certainly will get the chance to do some of that retrospective sensemaking when the police are interviewing you - and explain why you could not retreat and why you had to do what you had to do.

Whatever you do, make sure you can look back and know that you took every action with honor. Pat

Tillman was the quintessential honorable man. His story is up next. It is a good one.

The Pat Tillman Story

The long-haired, flip-flop wearing, football all-star from Arizona State University, Pat Tillman was known for his mental strength, indefatigable work ethic, and heart the size of Kansas. He was a terror to offensive players on the field and a monster in the classroom as well.

He was very close to what we would refer to as a Renaissance man today. He was strong, smart, savvy, and thoughtful. An unusually rare bird indeed. A combination of guts, glory, and genius. Pay close attention.

Pat Tillman was also known for climbing the light pole towers that illuminated the Arizona State University stadium during his time there.

He was introspective, philosophical, and interested in the roots of the very meaning of life while fully participating in the living of it. He was a man who had principles that undergirded his thoughts, words, and actions.

After the 9/11 terrorist attack in New York City, Tillman followed his heart and decided to forgo a multi-million dollar contract with the Arizona Cardinals to enlist in the United States Army.

Tillman became an elite Army Ranger. He was the quintessential soldier, demonstrating the highest levels of arete in his military duties. Akin to the arete he had shown on the college football gridiron stage and in his classrooms.

Even more interesting was Pat's detachment from the normal acquisitive nature that, all too often these days, haunts many people in the end. Many of us have storage units for our storage units. It is actually quite perverse.

Why do people ubiquitously seem to have such a compulsion to buy trinkets in the first place? Many of which they simply do not need and will never use, just to store away those goodies. Like little pack rats?

Pat Tillman would not have understood that way of being either. Pat was not materialistic. He kept it simple. Tillman knew that life had much more to offer than a few trinkets.

He fully lived his life in a manner that was conducive to creating his highest self and laser focused on his definite life purpose. Pat was a man of principles who was searching for meaning. He died an untimely death upon that honorable path.

Army Ranger Pat Tillman was killed in action in Afghanistan by what was later proved, after some spinning of the story, as "friendly fire."

Pat's way of being exemplified many, if not all, of the seven powerful fatherly lessons for raising healthy boys and healing broken men. He is a national treasure. He should be remembered and celebrated.

Pat was the perfect example of what we mean by going inward.

It has been instilled in you to look outward to the external experts to guide your decisions and tell you directly what to do. At this stage in your intellectual, emotional, and spiritual development, it is time to jettison that old way of being that is no longer serving you.

Now, you must awaken to the notion that you are responsible for your own health, your own wealth, and your own happiness. You are responsible. Moreover, know you can do this. To be successful you simply have to master one single solitary thing: yourself.

Self-mastery requires emotional control. The exercises in this book will assist you down the road of developing emotional control. Yet, the inner work that must be done is absolutely one hundred percent your own. A superb way to cultivate self-mastery is to learn the art of fasting.

You Are What You Eat Exercise 7: Learn to Fast

In Lesson Two, I broke down the deleterious nature of what I refer to as CRAP foods. The seventh You Are What You Eat exercise focuses on learning to fast.

"Sorry I lost my cool with you, dude. I was hangry."

Believe it or not, as of 2018, "hangry" is now a word in the Oxford English Dictionary.

Hangry is a relatively new type of word that actually tells us quite a bit about the nature of the world that we are now living in. People eat CRAP Frankenfoods that are horrible for them all day long. Most of them get really sick and drive up the cost of healthcare in the nation.

Obesity and overweightness is perhaps the most pressing and salient national, and even global, epidemic.

Now, we have new words to help us feel less responsible for the things we say or do.

How very stupid. How very weak.

Do not fall into the category of people who cannot conduct business as usual when they are hangry. You must condition yourself to remain responsible and at the helm of your own mind in terms of your thought processes, the things you say, and your physical actions. Get control of your taste buds by breaking your CRAP Frankenfood addictions. Eat sunlight foods. Once you have made the transition over to sunlight foods, consider adding a fasting exercise to your weekly training.

Fasting has been known throughout the ages to have health promotional benefits. Fasting is also a practice that has been employed by many different spiritual traditions all across the globe. Fasting confers spiritual benefits as well. Fasting provides a different perspective into my own self-realization work.

Do your research and know yourself well before getting on the fasting train. Again, fasting will come much easier once you have made the serious and sincere transition to a primary plant-based way of eating. Now, we are on to our workout exercise. Let us consider the health benefits of getting vertical. Onward we go to Workout Exercise Seven.

Workout Exercise 7: Get Vertical

Workout Exercise Seven focuses on getting vertical. At least one day a week, as you develop your own exercise routine based upon the ideas gleaned from this book, work in some vertical exercise time. Vertical exercises include any jumping exercises – from jumping on a trampoline to skipping rope to jumping on park benches – to rock or tree climbing.

Why should we get vertical?

All of these workouts require agility in one form or another. Whether that is balance, coordination, or decision making. You definitely need all three for rock and tree climbing!

The more agile you are in your workouts, the more agile you can be in all other parts of your life.

Also, if you want to look good in your suit or uniform, work some of these types of exercises into your weekly workout plan.

Park bench jumping is of course a free activity. Like always, be mindful of those around you in this situation like in any other public situation. Conduct yourself accordingly.

Start by standing in front of a park bench – facing the seat – with feet shoulder width apart. Then, you are going to want to either jump up onto the seat or step up onto it, one foot at a time. Be careful not to get the tip of your feet caught on the underside of the bench! Then you can either jump backwards to your starting position, if you are comfortable doing so, or step down. Know your limitations. Train to strengthen. Perfect form. Repeat eleven times.

If you want to take baby steps and work yourself up to jumping onto park benches, I recommend starting with starfish jumps. These are basically just park bench jumps without the park bench. Begin with feet shoulder width apart. Hold your arms close to your chest, almost as if you were typing on a computer. To initiate the move, simply squat and then explode up as high as you can jump, fully extending your body and spreading your arms and legs like a starfish. Fall back into a squat on your way down.

If you want to get into tree climbing, I highly suggest getting a good pair of work gloves, or actual tree climbing gloves, as tree bark can lacerate your hands.

I would know.

Be mindful of how you work your way up and down the tree and be careful with your footing and your grip.

This type of ascension and descension exercise is very good for sharpening your attention span. It is of the upmost importance not to fall obviously. You could also do pull-ups and other exercises in the tree. It is up to you and how far you want to push yourself during your weekly workout routine. Have at it and have fun.

Finally, for those of you looking to get out of the heat or out of the downpour, consider indoor rock climbing or indoor trampoline jumping. Both are great exercises that will increase your overall body strength, cardiovascular stamina, and provide darn near as close to a full body workout as you could ever hope to get in a traditional gym.

Meditation Exercise 7: Violet

Begin Meditation Exercise Seven with the pranayama warm-up. Your seventh energy center is found at the crown of your head. The color of this energy center is violet. It vibrates with the B note, and it is associated with the deadly sin of pride and the heavenly virtue of humility.

As you know well by now, finding the balance between these two is important.

We all know the types of people who exist on either end of the spectrum. Don't be either of those people. Wake up.

Find balance between these two poles as your career and life quality may well depend on you waking up to this issue immediately. See the purple energy sphere the size of a golf ball swirling at your crown center. Om the B note, either audibly or inaudibly, to awaken this energy center.

You know what to do. Grow your violet crown energy to the size of the orange and then to a basketball. Now with full force, Om until you surround your entire body with violet energy.

Ask for balance between the extremes of excessive pride and excessive humility. Reduce your B note, transmuting the violet cocoon down to the size of a basketball. Then, to the size of an orange. Finally, level down the Om vibrational intonation until it is the size of a golf ball.

Ask for balance in this and all areas of your bodily vessel.

The seventh note is begging now to be resolved. Start with the bottom red, low C note, and Om each of the succeeding notes until you finish the scale and climb up all of the energy centers. Come into equanimity, achieving simultaneous physical, emotional, and spiritual balance.

You feel an internal urge to complete the meditation by taking the entire vibrational intonation of the entire human bodily vessel upward one octave higher as you move from the B note to the C note. You long for this resolution.

So, give it to yourself. Get present. See your entire bodily vessel engulfed in a beautiful and radiant rainbow-colored sphere of harmony and balance. Resolution from dissonance is achieved through Oming the low C note one octave higher and envisioning your human bodily vessel surrounded in a healing white sphere that is bringing balance to your physical and emotional spiritual bodies. From C to shining C, your energy is balanced. You are ready. This is the end of the meditational exercises.

This is an exercise that can be done in multiple hour meditation sessions, or this approach can be used for quick tune ups in-between meetings at the office. It is up to you. Use the techniques in the ways that best serve your spiritual awakening and growth. Like all of the exercises presented in this book, use what works for you. Do some research of your own.

Modify these exercises in the ways that best serve you. Remember always that this book is a mere guide. You are ultimately responsible for the quality, character, and content of both your outer and inner worlds.

The more time that you spend in introspective meditational exercise, the better you will be able to handle, adapt to, and adjust trajectory to address the myriad vicissitudes and challenges that taking on a human bodily vessel will most certainly bring.

The Personal Strengths, Weaknesses, Opportunities, & Threats Analysis (SWOT Analysis) Exercise

This is the seventh of the seven exercises. You made it! In this final exercise, you will develop a personal strengths, weaknesses, opportunities, and threats analysis (SWOT analysis).

For this exercise, get out a piece of paper. Draw a large box with four squares. This is your matrix. In the top left corner box, write the word strengths. In the top right corner box, write the word weaknesses. In the bottom left corner box, write the word opportunities. In the bottom right corner box, write the word threats.

Write your strengths, your weaknesses, the opportunities you see on the horizon, and the threats you see on the horizon in the appropriate boxes. Step back. Examine the paper.

If you have been honest with yourself in your analysis, the sight before your eyes should be disconcerting and altogether uncomfortable to stomach. Hard truths about ourselves are often nauseatingly troublesome to our precious little egos. Tame the ego back.

See the reality about yourself as you exist today. Then, envisage the reality of the self that you will become by following the seven powerful fatherly lessons to achieve a divinely masculine way of being.

The matrix is a valuable tool that should be revisited often. As your life circumstances change for the better, if you are making decisions based upon the tools provided in this book, amend the matrix to accurately represent your current situation. You know your strengths.

Continue to build upon them. Try to move weaknesses to the strengths box. Try to eliminate threats and try to see opportunities in disguise.

Keep your head on a swivel, gentleman. Just because you have earned a degree, or some type of certification, that grants you the ability to do a job or trade today, it does not mean you will be at the top of your skill game tomorrow without continuous training and improvement.

Take life seriously, guys. Get as much training in your area of interest and expertise as possible.

That was it! You have completed the exercises in this book. Revisit them often. Keep this book on you at all times. Reference it when need be. Share the information contained herein regarding the true nature and magical majesty of the divinely masculine with other men and boys that cross your life existence path. They crossed your path for a reason.

We are all teachers. We are all students. Sharing the information presented in this book with others will bring joy, as well as a multitude of blessings, to your own life. Helping other men and boys to understand the seven powerful fatherly lessons for this dispensation will return untold benefits. Get to work. Do the exercises and meditational work presented in this book and you will begin to notice physical changes to and within your human bodily vessel.

As your vibrational frequency increases, walking the path of the divine masculine will become much more natural. Keep the end game of your spiritual evolution always in sight. Make sound and just decisions in life that will allow you to collect the necessary experiences that will catapult you forward both in this existence and the next. Blessings to each of you walking and sharing this path with others. In our conclusionary discussion, I leave you with elaboration upon divine masculinity and the art of self-reinvention.

Conclusion

Divine Masculinity & The Art Of Self-Reinvention

The lessons of this book cast light on much of the negative programming that has stultified men and boys emotionally, physically, intellectually, and spiritually. It is not too late to go inward and begin the magical journey of self-realization.

The divinely masculine directs sexual energy appropriately; eats sunlight foods; sows before expecting to reap; plays with heart; seeks to serve or disengage; covets self-understanding, self-reliance, and continuous self-refinement; and remains humble through the peaks and valleys of the human experience.

The divinely masculine man is a product of the synergistic force of the seven powerful fatherly lessons bequeathed to the world through this book.

As you begin to walk the path of the seven powerful fatherly lessons, your life will change. Remember, that this is the path towards emancipation, towards nirvana. It ain't always pretty, folks. The only way out is through.

It is never too late to get started on the path to strategic personal self-reinvention. You are worth it. Really, at this point, what do you really even have to lose? Let it be known that the divinely masculine path will not be easy. It will be worth it.

All in all, gentlemen, walking the path of the divinely masculine will be an arduous uphill battle, fraught with uncertainty, bringing forth unsolicited attacks from forces antithetical to the advancement of human freedom itself. Govern yourself accordingly.

The age of toxic Orwellian tribalism is readily upon us in full force today, my friends. The world has become increasingly anti-individualistic.

We are being forcibly fed a steady stream of lies both about ourselves and the world around us.

It is now time for us to wake up individually and begin helping others to awaken. Divine masculinity must now regain a strong foothold.

Divine Masculinity in the Age of Toxic Orwellian Tribalism

Picking up this book was no accident. You are on a spiritual journey. A journey fraught with myriad blockages, challenges, and obstacles that make room for exponential growth as you traverse the way. You are a spiritual traveler who has manifested a human bodily vessel for soul evolution in this lifetime. Wake up. Get to work. There is much to be done.

Depend on yourself. Learn to trust your gut. Keep your head up. Pay no attention to naysayers. This is your spiritual path. Your responsibility. Do not get distracted. Use technology wisely. Be wary of the spiritual stultification correlated with screen addiction. Distractions are spiritual pitfalls. Tests designed to divert you from the path. Put the phone down. Social media is the 'big daddy king' of all distractions.

Do the self-work instead. Jettison the negative voices from the past that have shackled you to suffering. Eradicate the old stories suppressing your bliss. Expose the numerous misconceptions that have long since hog-tied you to a reality of suffering as shams. Henceforth, you are responsible. Take the helm of your own mind. Start today.

Self-awareness is the first step. Begin to recognize the various and sundry forms of social engineering, and societal programming, that have led you to unquestionably lend credence to realities not serving your highest interest.

Much of this inculcation has been geared toward the creation of good little boys and girls. Consumers who do not ask too many questions so to speak. For example, eat the foods you see advertised on television. Take the pharmaceutical remedies to sustain eating said foods. How is that working out for us, folks?

Not surprisingly, 75% of American boys and men are overweight or obese. Many of those boys and men are taking record numbers of pharmaceutical drugs often for the amelioration of completely preventable diseases and ailments.

To compound and make matters worse, many of America's boys and men have become increasingly dependent on psychotropic drugs. That is just the legal, or the licit, side of the house. When you consider the prevalence of overdoses, from illegal opioids alone, I could rest my case forthwith. We are living within a garbage in, garbage out (GIGO) culture of consumption.

Stop purchasing goods and wares that you do not need.

The newest Louis Vuitton shirt, the latest cell phone or Apple watch, and the rest of the mundane trinkets that will all be obsolete soon enough. How is this working out for us? What is the payoff?

Americans are swimming in debt. Many of them owe their souls to the new company store, Amazon. Suffering abounds. We are living in a GIGO society.

What is the answer? How do I exit this GIGO matrix? Could you recommend a good Facebook spiritual guru? Should I pack my bags and fly off to an ashram in Bangladesh posthaste? Is meditation in a Himalayan cave required? No, no, and hell no. The answers are within you. You are the Holy Grail. Read on.

Life suffering is catalyzed by the misalignment of the seven energy centers located within the human bodily vessel.

1. Misalignment in our sex lives, perhaps in the shape of a pornographic addiction, stultifies the capacity to engage in healthy love-based sexual relationships.

2. Nutritional misalignment, perhaps in the form of gluttonous consumption of CRAP foods, is catching up to bariatric Westerners.

3. Consume, consume, consume. Conspicuous consumption, and programmed greed, are the new norms. All the while, ignoring the jewels of spiritual awakening within.

4. The insidious misalignment existing between the notions of expectation and effort. Everyone seems to want something for nothing these days. We don't sow.

5. Lies, lies, and more lies. When the content of one's character takes a back seat to the number of his or her social media followers, shooting straight is not valued. Does anyone have integrity today? Do you? Misalignment between word and deed is the primary source of many problems for many human beings in the world today personally, interpersonally, and societally.

6. Keeping up with the Joneses is tough sledding. Covetousness abounds. Veiled envy is today's dominant emotion lurking fastidiously beneath the surface of societal interactions. See the boiling cauldron of disgust, and utter visceral disdain, for your success, beneath the shiny veneer of your interlocutor's counterfeit smile. People will murder you today for your Air Jordan sneakers.

7. Sensationalism and unwarranted pretentiousness rule the day. Where can we find a little humility? It is rare. This is the epoch of ostentatiousness – on full display by the unabashedly oblivious – normalized and

legitimized through nightly inundations of reality television programming.

Does any of the above sound familiar? Take the helm of your own mind, body, and spirit. Determine where you are out of alignment and disconnected from both yourself and the world around you.

Become self-aware. Remember, self-correction only transpires after you have identified and recognized, said misalignments. Before that, you simply do not know what you do not know. Self-awareness necessarily precedes self-correction. Correspondingly, self-correction necessarily precedes self-realization.

Cultivate your bliss. Go inward. Go deep. Do the work of self-awareness, self-correction, and self-refinement. The joy of self-mastery has intrinsic rewards all its own. Know that the path of spiritual awakening is often a solitary journey. For many, it can be a rocky road.

Race, gender, creed, color, and ethnicity are blown all out of proportion, stultifying the collective consciousness in a manner that is overwhelmingly deleterious for the society at large.

The world is becoming increasingly tribalistic. It is actually all quite scary. Moreover, governments financed by big-tech oligarchs are being empowered with new Orwellian technologies, to include artificial intelligence, that are now capable of levels of intrusion into the daily lives of the citizenry at levels foreseen only by George Orwell himself.

The synergistic toxicity of oppressive technology and big corporation, should be disconcerting to all of us who have our critical thinking caps on. Yet, in all of this darkness, there remains a glimmer of hope on the horizon. Begin with you. Internalize, and really commit to exemplifying the seven new rules for societal interaction in each and every aspect of your life.

The Seven New Rules for Societal Interaction

Know yourself. Know your principles. Make principled decisions. Without further ado, here is a concise summation of the seven powerful fatherly lessons for this dispensation, in their distilled shorthand form.

1. Sexuality is Sacred
   Demonstrate Appropriate Sexual Behaviors at All Times
   Vet Partners
   Know the Costs of Fathering a Child
2. You Are What You Eat
   75% of Boys and Men, Are Overweight or Obese
   Eat Sunlight Foods
   You are Responsible for Your Own Health
3. Learn to Sow
   Sow Then Reap
   Depend on Your Own Hands
   Cultivate Arete in All Areas of Your Life
4. Play with Heart
   Diligence is The Great Equalizer
   Do Not Settle for Mediocre
   True Joy Results from Great Accomplishment
5. Serve or Disengage
   Make Use of Strategic Taciturnity
   Never Threaten Anyone for Any Reason
   Beware Your Digital Footprint
6. Covet Self Understanding
   Go Inward
   Learn to Trust Your Gut
   Seek Self-Realization
7. Strength Needs No Introduction
   Pursue Peace Through Strength
   Never Become Violent with Anyone for Any Reason (Except in Self-Defense)
   Serve, and Empower, Others as the Way of Strength

Respect for Thyself

The human bodily vessel is an instrument. One that very few tune consciously. More specifically, the human bodily vessel is an octave. A divine octave to be awakened. Valuable instruments are oft packaged, and delivered, with operator's manuals to ensure safe usage and effective operation. Should the priceless human bodily vessel instrument be any different? I think not.

Begin to reconceptualize your human bodily vessel as a treasured instrument. One of incalculable value. For that is precisely what it is, my friends.

This reconceptualization is both fundamental and foundational for the inner work of self-awareness and self-correction. It ultimately leads to self-realization. Know this now, you are the human octave. A divine instrument of grace. Think, act, and manifest accordingly. Tune.

Most people are seeking health, wealth, and happiness in this lifetime. Many don't know where to start.

The achievement of all three begins with the reconceptualization of the human bodily vessel as a one of a kind, irreplaceable, priceless instrument. Knowing you are worth the king's ransom oft curtails the introduction of toxic CRAP Frankenfoods, and mind-numbing media programming, into your Holy Grail. Take this reconceptualization to heart. This is square one. It is fundamental and axiomatic.

Prized violins have cases for their cases to ensure safe passage. Everyday use instruments, such as knives, require cleaning, sharpening, and stowage. It would be the acme of foolishness to assume that a dirty, dull knife, left out in the rain to rust, could serve its purpose. Instruments that are firing on all cylinders require care, protection, and upkeep.

This work has provided the reader with the requisite information, as well as a very foundational meditational toolkit, to start down the path of grounded reverence toward alchemic self-realization.

Meditative practices reduce life suffering. Meditative practices enhance one's physical, emotional, and spiritual resilience. Meditative practices are for you. Especially if you think that they are not for you. You are worthy. You are powerful. You are valuable. You deserve to walk this path.

Fortune favors the bold, my friends.

Respect yourself first and foremost by remembering that sex is sacred. That you are what you eat. Learn to sow. To play with heart. To serve or disengage. To covet self-realization and that strength needs no introduction. Self-respect is the prerequisite for all other respect. Begin with you. Start with respect for thyself. End with respect for thyself. Respect for others burgeons forth from the respect that one pays to thyself, my friends.

Respect for Others

Self-awareness entails checking in with your viscera as well as the other energy centers within your bodily vessel. Check in. What is pushing your buttons this day? Who is eating your lunch? What are you attached to that is the source of such worry? How are these things impacting how you are treating yourself and those in your radiance?

Self-correction entails identifying, and eradicating, errant thoughts connected with said energetic centers that curtail your greatness. Self-correction of your thinking, actions, and behaviors is a constant daily practice for the divinely masculine boy or man.

The endgame for each of us is self-realization. Self-realization has been conceptualized as Moksha in the Hindu faith, Samadhi in Buddhism, and the Christ Consciousness in the Judeo-Christian tradition. Self-realization is oft referred to as ascension.

You will often know where a human being is on the ascension path by observing how that human being treats other human beings. Take notice of how you yourself are indeed treating others, my friends. Show respect to everyone. All of the time.

In particular, take heed to respect women, and girls, at all times avoiding even the appearance of impropriety. Do not make cat calls. Do not speak to physicality in the academic environment, the workplace, or in any other public settings.

Respect for the other, in general, is quite easy to define. It is summed up by Lesson Five in this book entitled "Serve or Disengage." Say what you mean. Mean what you say. Do what you say. Take care to make use of strategic silence whenever appropriate.

There is no conferred advantage to broadcasting, or livestreaming, your opinions, aches and pains, or other political identity types or gripes to the world. No one cares.

Moreover, never threaten or go to fisticuffs with anyone, for any reason, except in extremely rare cases of necessary self-defense. Even then, think twice.

A good rule to live by, henceforth, is to never put your hands on anyone in acts of intimidation or physical violence.

Use guns and knives, appropriately. For self-defense purposes only. Know the firearm laws where you live. Never brandish a firearm unless you plan to use it. Only plan to use a firearm, or other deadly or injurious weapon, in a case of serious self-defense where retreat is not an option.

If those firearm laws are too restrictive for your tastes, run for public office. Change the state statutes, the local ordinances, or just move to a place that is better suited for your own 2nd Amendment self-protection.

As far as the amorous relationships go, date outside of your school, work, and training environments. Your gym and yoga studios are training environments, gentlemen. Stay focused. Keep your eyes on the prize.

If you are in school, focus on school. Not relationships. There will be time for relationships once you have achieved your educational goals.

When you do date, if you decide to become sexually active, do so with the sober consent of a highly vetted partner for whom you have immense trust.

Spreading yourself too thin with multiple sexual partners proves to often be the absolute and total downfall of many unsuspecting, and unwary, boys and men.

In the age of toxic tribalism and by the very nature of the testosterone that runs through your veins, you have a target on your back.

Do not give the provocateurs any legitimate reason to come after you. Shield yourself from the toxicity, my friends. Embody the seven powerful fatherly lessons in your very way of being to achieve liberation in this very lifetime.

Live it.

Embodying the Seven Powerful Fatherly Lessons in Your Way of Being

The very premise of this book is that you should begin to take the helm of your own mind through a self-realization awakening of your perception of the energetic centers within your own human bodily vessel.

These energy centers will run on autopilot, primarily driven by the inculcated programming that we have all received through the years. If you want to live a more awakened and full life to really experience all you can be in your human bodily vessel, you must ultimately take responsibility for your own energy flow in terms of frequency and intensity of vibration.

You are a brilliant pillar of light, shining brightly to the heavens and beyond.

Know that you are an instrument. Like all other instruments, you too need tuning. This book has provided some foundational meditative practices to kickstart your meditative path. Do your own meditative practice. Share what you learn with others.

As you re-read the chapter content of this book, and practice the daily meditations herein, you will learn to consciously amplify and de-amplify the frequency and intensity of sounds and colors that constitute each of the seven primary energy centers within your own human bodily vessel instrument.

Cultivating the ability to self-regulate the intensity and frequency of your own human bodily instrument will allow you to live free from many of your current limitations.

Your awareness of how your creative abilities shape and reshape the reality in which you live will be enhanced as you gain command over the self-regulation of the energy centers located within your very own body.

This book has introduced the reader to daily practices of attunement that, when practiced in earnest, will catalyze and invigorate massive spiritual growth in this lifetime.

Your new way of being will be conducive to whatever achievements, goals, or desires that you want to see manifest in your life. The work that is ahead is highly pragmatic.

The upside: It works!

The downsides: It is expensive, it is going to suck, and you are going to hate it.

None of those downsides are actually true to reality. Although you may be quite convinced of such for a time in the beginning!

Understand that, from this point forward, you are responsible for your own mental, physical, and spiritual health. The self-awareness, self-correction, and self-realization exercises found at the conclusion of each of the chapters herein have set the intention for your attainment of optimal levels of health, wealth, and happiness in this lifetime. Carry out the work necessary to bring that intention into fruition. Energetic self-realization toward the attainment of one's highest potential is the endgame of the path of the divinely masculine boy or man. It is truly up to you to save your own life!

Let the real work of pragmatic spiritual growth begin for you in earnest with the multitude of blessings bestowed on the near horizon. Stay on path. Stay on the horse. Stay the course.

Take the time now to re-read the chapters in this book with renewed enthusiasm.

Living the seven powerful fatherly lessons for raising healthy boys and mending broken men will manifest demonstrable, direct improvements in your health, finances, and overall state of life happiness.

Remember knowledge is power. The information and exercises in this book, when applied in concert, contain the synergistic power to save your life. Go inward. Go deep. Enjoy the ride.

There are a boatload of guru sharks, politicians, and snake oil salespeople all trying to get you to drink their Kool-Aid. Spit it out. Those concoctions will only serve to steer you away from divine masculinity. See the traps set before you. Awaken.

Follow the seven powerful fatherly lessons and you shall be offered a shield of divine protection.

Make up your own mind about how you are going to live your life and with whom you are going to interact, in both business and personal matters. Your time is your own.

Change the nouns – the people, the places, and the things – in your life if they are no longer serving your highest interest. Misery or bliss, it is on you.

The government is not going to raise healthy boys nor mend broken men. Nonprofit agencies are not going to raise healthy boys nor mend broken men. Churches are not going to raise healthy boys nor mend broken men.

If healthy boys are to be raised and broken men are to be mended, it is on us, my friends. We boys and men have to do this for ourselves. It is what we should have been doing all along.

About the Author

Matthew Lloyd Collins was born in Opelika, Alabama. Raised on the Eastern Shore of Virginia in the tiny Chesapeake Bay hamlet of Onancock, Collins grew up working in the agriculture and commercial fishing industries.

Collins earned both his bachelor's and master's degrees in public administration at Virginia Commonwealth University (VCU). Collins earned his PhD in public administration and public policy at Virginia Tech (VT). Professionally, Collins has served as a deputy county administrator, county administrator, public policy analyst, college professor, and consultant.

At the age of forty, Collins experienced a profound spiritual awakening. Today, Matthew Lloyd Collins is an author, spiritual teacher, podcast host, and nonprofit 501 (c) 3 organization executive director.

Collins teaches yoga and meditation inside the jails and prisons of North Florida. Collins also teaches "Making Men Workshops" for boys and "The Awakened Man Workshops" for men.

Both workshops are offered face-to-face and online. Email Collins directly for workshop information at DMLCShow@Gmail.com.

The Dr. Matthew Lloyd Collins Show is a nonprofit 501 (c) 3 organization. You can visit the show's website at www.DMLCShow.com.